THE AUTOBIOGRAPHY OF
# RODERICK C. MEREDITH
*Called to Do God's Work*

# Contents

**Forward**   i

**Preface:** Used for the Work of God   1

**Chapter 1:** Roots of Faith   5

**Chapter 2:** Seeking Truth   19

**Chapter 3:** Embracing God's Calling   29

**Chapter 4:** Early Ministry   39

**Chapter 5:** Priceless Opportunities   47

**Chapter 6:** Building a Family and Foundation   55

**Chapter 7:** Trials and Encouragement   63

**Chapter 8:** Expanding Horizons   71

**Chapter 9:** The Work Moves Forward   81

**Epilogue:** The Big Picture   88

**Afterword**   91

RCM Edition 1.0 | June 2024
©2024 Living Church of God™
All rights reserved. Printed in the U.S.A.

**This booklet is not to be sold!**
It has been provided as a free public educational service by the Living Church of God.

All Scripture quotations, unless otherwise indicated, are taken from the *New King James Version* (© 1982 by Thomas Nelson, Inc.). Used by permission. All rights reserved.

# Roderick C. Meredith
## 1930-2017

*Foreword by Gerald E. Weston*

The first time I met Dr. Roderick C. Meredith was in 1965 at the faculty reception for the incoming freshman class at Ambassador College. I had read some of his articles in *The Plain Truth* magazine, but had little idea of the caliber of man he was. At the time, he was not outwardly impressive. He was a very young-looking 35-year-old, of a small build and with thick glasses. As is often the case, you cannot tell a book by its cover. Those glasses and youthful look belied the dynamo inside.

The last time we met, he was a frail 87-year-old man with only days to live. But long before then, I had come to realize the greatness of this man of God. In those intervening years, we had crossed paths many times. I was always the student, and he was my teacher. He was a valued advisor to Mr. Herbert W. Armstrong, a superintendent of ministers, a powerful speaker, and an insightful writer. And he was a dear friend.

In many ways, this autobiography is about *two* great men. You cannot read this work without realizing how profoundly Herbert Armstrong shaped Dr. Meredith's adult life. And the closer we get to another person—especially one we have looked up to—the more we realize that there was only one perfect person ever to walk this earth. I was close enough to both Mr. Armstrong and Dr. Meredith to realize that neither was perfect. Each had shortcomings, alongside so many visible strengths and gifts from God. Yet one theme defined them both: their sincere desire and effort to obey and serve their Creator above all else. They feared God more than man.

Even some of Dr. Meredith's detractors openly admitted that he was what we might call "the real deal." He was what he professed to be. He believed what he taught—and he lived it, with God's help, to the best of his ability.

After Mr. Armstrong's death, his successor, Joseph Tkach, took the Worldwide Church of God in a very different direction, turning away from true Christianity and adopting the world's paganized Protestantism. The changes took place so quickly that tens of thousands of faithful members were left in confusion. Some consider the appointment of Mr. Tkach to be a catastrophic mistake made by Mr. Armstrong, but we can understand that the true Head of the Church, Jesus Christ, let this test come on the Church to reveal who was truly "with it" and who was merely a pretender.

Dr. Meredith had devoted his entire adult life to the Church of God, and he sought to remain faithful. Yet he came to see that the corporate body of the Church had apostatized and that there would be no turning back. At age 62, when most men are beginning to think about retirement, the apostates offered him a comfortable retirement package to keep quiet. But those who hoped he would take the offer never understood the man. As one of the first evangelists Mr. Armstrong had ordained, Dr. Meredith recognized his responsibility to revive the Work that God had raised up through his mentor.

Starting with just a handful of brethren faithful to God's truth and the Work of the Church—there were just 19 at the first Sabbath service of the Global Church of God—Dr. Meredith quickly established a radio program and then a television program. He began publishing a new magazine and writing booklets proclaiming the truth of God. And all of it was done with the speed and purpose that those who knew Dr. Meredith had come to expect of this dedicated servant of God. For this, and much more, so many of us in the Church of God, including my wife and me, were grateful then and remain grateful today.

In retrospect, we can see how God gave special preparation to a young man from Joplin, Missouri. At a young age, he was given the opportunity to travel and see that the world was much greater than his hometown—or even his college town. We can see this genesis of a world vision in his description of his first trip abroad. God also gave him special preparation as an early pioneer student at Ambassador College where, even while still a student, he helped build the expanding Work that God was accomplishing through Mr. Armstrong, his mentor and another man of vision and unique preparation. When apostasy rocked Worldwide after Mr. Armstrong's death, few if any others had the biblical knowledge—and the writing, speaking, and organizational skills—to do the Work that needed to be done. And no other had the determination and drive to do what Dr. Meredith did.

Dr. Meredith never saw the Church as a means of taking care of himself. He focused with vision and determination on the great commission Christ gave to all His future servants—to proclaim to the whole world the Gospel of the coming Kingdom of God and to give the Ezekiel warning to the Israelite peoples. And he worked tirelessly to instill in others the vision and determination he had absorbed from his mentor, Mr. Armstrong—in which we in the Living Church of God strive to continue today.

Dr. Meredith was always quick to remind us that, despite his role of leadership, the Work was not about him, but about serving God. He understood that God had prepared him for the task at hand, but he knew he was no greater than other men. And God could not have used Dr. Meredith if he were not deeply converted. His focus, apart from the great commission, was to feed on Christ, absorb His words, and draw near to Him in prayer, study, meditation, and fasting. Those close to him saw him set this example in his way of life.

Every life is important, and every life has its own history. The life story of Roderick C. Meredith is important not just because of what he did as one man, but because his life was immersed for nearly 70 years in the most important work being done on earth. As Mr. Richard Ames once remarked, Dr. Meredith *was* history.

The day will soon come when the resurrected saints of God will meet together in the air. We look forward to our reunion then with Dr. Meredith, when he will hear the most encouraging words a saint can hear from his Creator: "Well done, good and faithful servant!"

# Preface
## Used for the Work of God

Because God's true Church was harassed, persecuted, and scattered, it was virtually unknown to most of the world until the middle of the twentieth century. At that time, Almighty God raised up a remarkable man, Mr. Herbert W. Armstrong, and used him to reinvigorate His true Church and infuse it with a sense of zeal and purpose far beyond what it had carried before under weak, uncertain leadership.

As enormous end-time prophetic events begin to change our nations and our very lives, it will become increasingly obvious to those whom God is calling that Mr. Armstrong was used to explain specific *prophecies* of what was to happen at the time of the end *far* more than any other man. No one else even comes *close*. Billy Graham, Oral Roberts, Jerry Falwell, and all the other "prophecy preachers" never talked or gave specific details about the downfall of America and Britain, the loss of our great "sea gates," the exit of the Soviet forces from Eastern European countries, the reunification of Germany, the "take-down" of the Berlin Wall, and all the other events that Mr. Armstrong talked about in his writings and teachings *long* before they happened.

As the end-time leader of the Church of God—God's body of people so named twelve times in the New Testament—Mr. Armstrong was used by God to make clear many of the details of the Creator's intervention in human affairs. These were not "done in a corner" (Acts 26:26). These events should show all of us that God is real, for He *is* beginning to intervene in human affairs more than He has at any other time in recent centuries.

# The Autobiography of Roderick C. Meredith

So, it was an honor and privilege for me, as a young man from Joplin, Missouri, to somehow be brought by God to Ambassador College to be one of the "pioneer students" and later one of the evangelists helping Mr. Armstrong raise up this present end-time Work. The Church was just beginning to grow when I came to Ambassador College in 1949. We only had three local congregations—Portland, Eugene, and Pasadena. There were *no* congregations east of the Rockies and brethren were still few in number—scattered around the United States and desiring to have more direct help. Yet Mr. Armstrong was only one man and not able to provide that personal leadership until he raised up Ambassador College for the purpose of training more leaders to help the Work grow. And I had the honor and opportunity to be a part of that very effort. When I came to the Church, there were just a few hundred members, and when I graduated in 1952 there were still only a few hundred members. But God used me, along with others, to help Mr. Armstrong publish the magazines in a steady fashion, conduct nationwide baptizing tours, raise up congregations, and otherwise build the Work in a way that one man alone was not able to do. This was not to our credit, but to the credit of the living Jesus Christ, who guided Mr. Armstrong to train faithful men who would be able to carry on the Work and help it grow. Through Mr. Armstrong's leadership, the Church grew to an attendance of 150,000 members with scores of congregations, *The Plain Truth* magazine achieved a circulation of 8.3 million subscribers, and a radio/TV audience of countless *millions* of human beings around the world was reached.

For several years, I was regarded as the "third man" in the Work—behind Mr. Armstrong and his son Garner Ted—being given the title "Second Vice President." I was able to teach Ambassador College Bible classes and raise up congregations in the early years, I was the only one to serve as Deputy Chancellor of all three campuses of Ambassador College, and I had many other privileges in helping Mr. Armstrong build the Work. None of this makes me better in my spiritual situation, and I certainly do not claim this or feel this way at all. But as one who spent *thousands* of hours with Mr. Armstrong and was regarded in a certain way as a "third son" with whom he would share in heartfelt detail his attitudes, his problems, and his challenges, I can give insight into what happened in the early days in *addition* to the wonderful information contained in Mr. Armstrong's own autobiography.

# Preface

As I was reflecting on this one day at lunch, one of our leading ministers, Mr. Richard Ames, made an encouraging comment when I was talking about my having a great personal knowledge of the recent history of the Church: "Rod," he said, "you *are* history!" I honestly had more personal opportunity—in God's mercy—to get to know Mr. and Mrs. Herbert Armstrong and their family than any other human being still alive today as I write this. So, I can give you insights and help you understand the real history and background of what really got the Work going in those days of which we are now a continuation in the Living Church of God with the Work of *Tomorrow's World*. These special insights should help you see the "big picture" in understanding the events around you, how God is working in His true Church today, and what you *personally* ought to be doing.

I hope that this will be helpful to all of you who read this. I pray that you will be able to look *beyond* the human nature of human beings. May God help you to see the "big picture" and "walk with God," more assured than ever that He is real, that He is working out a purpose here below, and that He *does* have a true Church and true servants on this earth today. And I want you to truly understand that God has *always* used weak, sinful human beings to do His Work. Even King David, a man after God's heart (Acts 13:22), had massive human failures. Yet God looked on his heart and used him because of his passion to honor God, worship Him, and serve Him. That is exactly what we in this Work have tried to do. You need to *understand* that attitude and follow it as *awesome* and prophetic events begin to move forward swiftly in the years just ahead of us.

May God help all of you who read this to do so with an *open* mind and to want to really learn where the Creator has worked and is *now* working in reaching this world with His true message today—at the time of the end.

Preparing to board the boat to England in the spring of 1960 with son Michael in his arms and daughter Elizabeth at his side

# Chapter 1

## Roots of Faith

The big ship seemed to shudder as we passed the Statue of Liberty, for the Queen Elizabeth's huge engines took over as the tugboats left us and we moved out to sea. Just then, the ship's huge fog horns blasted loudly, sending a chill up and down my spine. I was leaving the United States of America for the first time.

It was truly exciting to be onboard the largest ocean liner on earth and be heading out to the open sea, for Richard David Armstrong and I were sailing to England. This was definitely one of the greatest life-changing experiences for me, and it enlarged my horizons even more than I had imagined it would.

Here I was, Rod Meredith from Joplin—a comparatively small city in Southwest Missouri. If I had stayed in Joplin or in that area, as many of my friends did, I would never remotely have had the remarkable experiences that came my way. I would probably have never truly understood *why* I was born, what the *purpose* of human life really is, or the real *meaning* of the swiftly moving prophetic events that are even now beginning to occur. But even from my teenage years, I had wanted to understand the meaning of *life*. In my own youthful way, I began to study, to meditate, and to pray and seek God's help in understanding the ultimate questions of life. That earnest quest had led me all the way from Southwest Missouri to Ambassador College in Pasadena, California. And now, I was about to be in England.

I was born in Freeman Hospital in Joplin, Missouri, on June 21, 1930. My parents and grandparents were all mainstream Protestants, and my grandmother was even Superintendent of Sunday Schools at one time. Both my parents were graduates of a Methodist college, Baker University in Baldwin City, Kansas. My paternal grandfather, C.D. Meredith, was also college-educated and became Deputy State Veterinarian, followed in this responsibility by his son, C. Paul Meredith, my father's younger brother.

My maternal grandfather, Timothy Keohane, came from Ireland and settled in Kansas where he married Hannah Sophia McNeil, a woman of mainly English stock. They produced a family of eight children—seven girls and one boy. The "Keohane sisters" nearly all became teachers, primarily in English, literature, and related subjects.

My Grandfather Keohane was Mayor of the city of Baldwin, Kansas, for a time and often participated in a debating society in that area. My mother told me that they had "fiery" debates over religion and other similar topics during those years. "Political correctness" had not yet arrived.

One interesting side note involves C.D. Meredith and his wife, my paternal grandmother, the former Elizabeth Cunningham. When they left northern Missouri, Elizabeth's mother was afraid that the couple would end up in Indian Territory. She had said over and over that she was afraid to go there and would *not* live in Indian Territory. But C.D. brought her down in a covered wagon—crossing quietly across the border, since there *was* no real marked border—and after three days informed her that they had *already* been in Oklahoma (the area had recently become U.S. territory) for three days.

That is where my father grew up—in a town called Afton, Oklahoma. But the opportunity to enlarge his veterinary practice caused my Grandfather Meredith to move up to Joplin, Missouri, a swiftly growing mining town. My grandfather's practice prospered, and he also owned and operated a livery stable for some time, where he was able to hang out at night and talk to his buddies, avoiding a lot of "religious talk" from my deeply religious grandmother.

After my parents, Henry Carl Meredith and Mildred Keohane, met and married at Baker University in Kansas, they moved to my father's hometown, Joplin, and he became an accountant for Browning Buick Company. After that firm went bankrupt during the Great Depression, he ended up working for his father as an accountant and as "Assistant Veterinarian"—often doing full veterinarian work such as vaccinations under his father's direction.

After I was born, our first home was at 512 Empire Street in Joplin. It was a comparatively small brick home, which still looks pretty good today, as it is *all* brick. As my two sisters came along—Patricia, nearly three years later, and Kathryn, about five-and-a-half years later—I was forced to move for a few years to the couch in our living room. So, because of the Depression and other circumstances, I grew up in a somewhat humble environment. But we always had *plenty* to eat, my father had a car and regular job, and I was not aware that we were in *any* way suffering.

As I matured, I saw men all over town who were out of work or who were working for the "WPA"—the Works Project Administration, which President Franklin Roosevelt had established to give men something to do. It made me thankful that my father did have a job and that we had a pretty good, mainly middle-class life despite the tight financial conditions all around us. However, as I look back, it probably did me good to grow up in humble circumstances—having to sleep on the couch and not having my own private room, as my own children all had later. The need to work *hard* and get things done was always paramount in my mind as I grew up during the Great Depression and World War II.

## My Early Training

I attended grade school in Joplin and deeply enjoyed life at that time. But all of us "normal" boys got into trouble from time to time and acted up more than we should have. I remember that many of us were pulling the girls' pigtails and tickling them as we would come in from the school playground. They would squeal and yell and make lots of noise. There was a lot of obstructiveness at various activities as our school principal, a very old lady, was not able to do much.

However, one day we sadly lost our principal, mainly because of old age. But a *new* principal—a young, vigorous man named Paul Antle—had been appointed. Soon after that, as we were coming in from a recess with our usual noisy jiggling, pigtail pulling, and obstructiveness, I suddenly heard a frantic yelp from a boy in the line behind me. I turned and beheld Mr. Antle with a large wooden paddle coming down hard on this boy's behind. All of us little boys *instantly* straightened up at attention and became very quiet. From then on, great peace descended upon West Central Grade School.

Mr. Antle was a good man, but in those days, teachers were allowed to maintain discipline—so he did, firmly and fairly. All of us boys came to respect him, as did the girls. And being younger and more up to date, he was a very good administrator.

I shall never forget how our entire grade school was brought into the school auditorium on December 8, 1941, just after Japan had attacked Pearl Harbor. A large radio was set up on the stage with old-fashioned speakers attached to it so the entire student body could hear the address to Congress by President Franklin Delano Roosevelt—declaring war on Japan. It was indeed *stirring* to hear this address, which he concluded with the words, "We shall gain the inevitable triumph, so help us *God*." All of us students could sense that "something different" was happening around us. Our parents had become very sober on the previous day, Sunday, when the news of the Japanese attack had been announced. *Everything* was changed.

We were soon busy collecting tin foil and scrap metal to help in the war effort and were involved in "winning the war" in more ways than one. It was an entirely different spirit than the later atmosphere during the Korean War and the Vietnam War, for nearly *everyone* was patriotically involved. We stood straight and proud when the National Anthem was played at most occasions. We knew that we *were* going to win, no matter what. It was a time to grow up with the right kind of *soberness* and *purpose* in our lives.

Although our family went to church regularly on Sunday, we did take off every month or so to go to our cabin down in the woods. My father owned a cabin on top of a big hill overlooking Elk River near Noel, Missouri. It was an area so picturesque that filmmakers chose it as the place to film the old movie *The Return of Frank James*. I had *wonderful* times hiking in the woods and going up and down the river, mainly fishing with my father in his big rowboat. My father, although not a big man, was a very muscular man. He had spent a lot of time doing various exercises, especially on the parallel bars. So, he was able to chin himself three times with *just* his right arm. Very few men are able to do that at *any* age. Anyway, being with my father in those and many other occasions helped me develop my sense of masculinity as I saw how he faced outdoor situations and handled himself even during difficult times.

Once, when we were walking along the edge of the river, he stepped on a rusty nail that went way up into his foot, giving him a great deal of pain and causing blood to begin to seep out into his tennis shoe. I will always remember—still being a little guy of only six or eight years old—sitting there and hoping that it would be "okay." My dad was hurting, breathing heavily, and bleeding, but I heard him mutter, "I've got to get going and get Roddy back up that hill." In spite of the pain, he took my hand firmly and, limping as he went, helped pull me back up the hill to our cabin where my mother was able to bathe and cleanse the wound and put in turpentine or something. It seemed that in nearly every situation, my dad proved himself to be "all man." He told me to learn to be "tough." So, although I was never big in stature—later growing to 5 foot 10½ in height and about 150 pounds—I learned to use what strength I had to the very best of my ability and tried to face life fearlessly. My dad bought me boxing gloves as a little boy, taught me to exercise regularly, and took me out on long walks and hikes.

We also went camping occasionally, sleeping in tents down by Shoal Creek, Elk River, and other beautiful areas there in Southwest Missouri. I shall always remember sitting around the campfire with my father and his friend Bill Ditson, and hearing them tell tales about their youthful exploits, "tough guy" experiences, etc. Some of my happiest experiences were with my family at our cabin and on such camping trips as I have just described. The outdoors has always had a great appeal to me, and I deeply feel that anyone who has not spent a lot of time out in God's creation has missed out on a great deal.

## My Many Friends

In our own neighborhood in town, there were a *lot* of boys. Even our mothers remarked that it seemed that so many women were having boys rather than girls at that particular point in time. I had a group of 25 male friends—all of whom I could name today and most of whom lived in places that I can still remember. Because of our enthusiasm for life, our athletic ability, and the fact that we were all about the same age, our group really bonded in those youthful days of grade school, junior high school, and high school.

To this day, I can recall again and again the *wonderful* times I had with Jimmy Mallett, Jimmy Porter, Ashby Grantham, "Ducky"

McPherson, Monty Taylor, and many others. Our "gang," both boys and girls, would go roaring around the neighborhood on long summer evenings chasing after each other as we played hide-and-seek or kick-the-can, or similar games. Later, in junior high, we boys would sometimes venture clear out to the edge of town to a local cemetery where some would have gone ahead so they could frighten us by suddenly *leaping out* from behind the gravestones. Often, after seeing a "thriller" movie like *Frankenstein Meets the Wolf Man*, we would get together in our friends' backyards—perhaps sleeping out on cots during hot weather—and try to frighten each other in various ways. But, as I have related, once the Pearl Harbor attack took place, a sense of soberness came over us, even more than would have been the case otherwise, for we were all *Americans*. We were thankful for our country and *proud* of it, and we all wanted to learn to be *strong*—physically, mentally, and emotionally.

Yet we enjoyed many delightful experiences during junior high and senior high with sports, dances, parties, and all kinds of wonderful activities. Though I was certainly not the tallest player, I was a leader on our junior high basketball team when we played one of the other junior high teams for a local championship of some sort. At the half-time of one championship game, our team went dejectedly down to the basement locker rooms—we were behind by quite a few points.

Even then, I had begun to realize that there was a real *God,* and I prayed to Him occasionally. Waiting until all the fellows had gone back up (so I thought), I got down on my knees briefly and asked God in *prayer* to please help us win this game. As I came to the foot of the stairway to go back up to the basketball court, I encountered John Ivey, who, unknown to me, had also stayed behind. I think there were tears in both of our eyes. I said, "John, have you been praying?" He nodded. So, we went staunchly up to the basketball court and did our very best to win. John was somewhat taller and a better basketball player, and he ended up pouring in basket after basket and getting us up to a tie with the other team, so we had to go into overtime. In overtime, we were still tied until, somehow, just before the buzzer, I grabbed the ball away from the opposition and threw it—just like a baseball—at the basket. It went in.

So, I made the winning score, and John, who had also prayed, made far more baskets than I did. Both of us talked about it soberly later and I am sure that it helped us to understand the *reality* of our Father in heaven, even at that youthful age.

## Maturing Experiences

Meanwhile, however, I received a great deal of help and encouragement along this line from my paternal grandmother, Elizabeth Cunningham Meredith. She was a *very* religious Methodist and sincerely studied and tried to understand the Bible in her own way. From when I was about age six and for about ten years, I quite often went over to her house, as it was just a few blocks away—she took me in and gave me cookies, hot chocolate, and lots of love. But she also read the *Bible* to me directly, in a way no one ever did before or since. She got me interested in what the Bible actually *says*. She did not fully understand the need to obey our Creator, nor did she understand *anything* about prophecy. But she showed me, in her own way, that the Bible made sense and was an *extremely* helpful book about life and the purpose of life. I can never forget the long hours I spent with Grandmother talking about those things and her directly reading the Bible to me in that way. It helped me then, and it has helped me ever since in my life and walk with God.

During the summer of 1945, as World War II was winding down, my parents sent me up to northern Kansas to work on a rather large wheat farm owned by Mr. Ward Henry. They had arranged for me to work there through my mother's sister's husband, who was the "country banker" in Robinson, Kansas. Since Uncle Milward Idol loaned money to these farmers, they were somewhat indebted to him and, besides, in that small community they were all friends. My older cousin, Bob Idol, had worked on the same farm years before, and it was a *wonderful* experience for me to be up there—nearly 200 miles from home—working all day long on this big wheat farm, learning skills and having experiences I never would have had in the same way as a "city boy" back in Joplin.

Since I was big for my age, I looked a little older than I was. And I wore a "US Marine" tee-shirt into town from time to time. On one occasion, an older man came up and asked me if I had "just come back from the war." I had to admit to him, sheepishly, that I was only 15 years old. But it made me feel *proud* to be associated with the United States Marines, for I had literally run away from home for a couple of weeks about six months earlier in a sort of "teenage moment" to try to prove my masculinity by joining the Marines—but I had been sent home.

At the end of that summer on the farm, now back home in Joplin, I woke up one morning and went down to breakfast—we had moved to a larger, two-story framed home in a better neighborhood by then—and found my dad staring at the local paper more intently than usual. My dad was a man of few words, but, this time, I knew that something was up, for he gave me a little talk about how all things in life change and how "the sun still comes up the next morning."

Then he handed me our local paper, *The Joplin Globe*. There, on the front of the society section, was the notice that Jimmy Mallett, son of prosecuting attorney Russell Mallett, had just had his neck broken in a wrestling accident and had died in the ring right in front of his own parents. It especially *shook* me to the depths of my being, for Jimmy was one of my best friends and he and I had wrestled for *hours* in our families' backyards and other places during the long summers—like two little bear cubs rolling around in the grass, trying out *jujitsu* "tricks" on each other and practicing various wrestling holds—testing ourselves against each other, as little boys often do.

I was asked to be a pallbearer at Jimmy's funeral a few days later. In those days, they sometimes lowered the coffin right into the ground soon after the funeral. As I watched Jimmy's body being lowered into the ground, I *very* soberly thought to myself about how *short* life is. And, over and over, I wondered, "*Why* did God let Jimmy die?" Jimmy and I had played together, wrestled together, and had long philosophical talks about the meaning of life. We had even written off to a guy named "Dingle" out in Los Angeles who'd had a little ad in the paper about learning the "Wisdom of the East." We found that his ideas were kind of nebulous, but we still thought and talked about *why* we were born and what life was all about.

### I WONDER

If I could only know
Which way the winds do blow
When the sun comes over the hill.
If I could only see
A vision of me
Twenty-five years from today.
If I could only find
What my questioning mind
Would like so much to know.
If I could only dream
A dream that would seem
To tell me the mysteries of life.
If I could only learn
What makes the world turn
A happier man I would be,
Then I wouldn't die sad,
For my heart would be glad
To see what my eyes couldn't see.

                                    Roderick Meredith

A poem he wrote while a student at Joplin High School

# The Autobiography of Roderick C. Meredith

ca. 1931

At the family cabin ca. 1936

Age 2

Age 9, in front of his home at 512 Empire Street in Joplin, Kansas

C.D. & Elizabeth Meredith (far left, third from left) with C. Paul & Ethel Meredith (far right) and Elizabeth's sister (second from left)

ca. 1933

Age 8, with sister Patricia (age 5)

# The Autobiography of Roderick C. Meredith

Age 6 (far left), with parents Henry and Mildred and sisters Patricia (age 3) and Kathryn (2 months)

ca. 1932

With sisters Patricia and Kathryn ca. 1940

Dr. C.D. & Elizabeth Meredith with their sons
Henry Carl (age 11) and Clarence Paul (age 6)

Henry Carl Meredith and the
former Mildred Keohane on their
wedding day, June 14, 1925

Competing in the mile run at Joplin High School, 1947

## Chapter 2

### Seeking Truth

From this time on, after Jimmy's death, I began a quest to—even more than ever—try to *understand* the meaning of life, *if* there was a real God, and what it was all about. Jimmy was gone, but, as they say, "life moves on," and I was a kid still having a lot of activities and youthful—even happy—experiences, though the "meaning of life" question was always in the back of my mind. I realized that I was still pretty skinny, and I wanted to be big and strong and a powerful athlete in high school and college. So, during the latter part of junior high school, I talked my father's younger brother, C. Paul Meredith, into joining me in buying a York "Big 12" barbell and weightlifting set. We lifted weights nearly every night in Uncle Paul's very well-kept garage with a concrete floor. Afterwards, he would invite me upstairs to his apartment where he and his wife, Aunt Ethel, would listen to the radio together in the evenings. Remember, there was *no* television in those days.

Uncle Paul was also beginning to be deeply interested in the meaning of life, so he would turn on the radio to the programs of various radio preachers, trying to find real *answers*. After hearing quite a few of them, we narrowed our interest down to Herbert W. Armstrong and one other minister, both of whom seemed to make much more sense than the others. Finally, it became clear that only Herbert W. Armstrong *really* understood the Bible and was able to explain specifically the meaning of prophecy, the meaning of life, and many other things that are so generalized in mainstream religion that they often become

## The Autobiography of Roderick C. Meredith

Dr. C. Paul Meredith's home ca. 1947, where he and his nephew Rod would listen to Mr. Armstrong on the radio

somewhat meaningless. I continued hearing Mr. Armstrong, off and on, from the autumn of 1944 until the end of his life.

But the excitement of high school activities beckoned, and I certainly poured myself into them with great enthusiasm and a fair amount of joy and success. For a while, I played on the football team and the basketball team and ended up being the "star" mile runner on the Joplin High School track team. I continued football all the way through high school, but I was never a "star," as I was a little thinner than average and had to wear glasses—and, later on, contact lenses—so I could see which guy to tackle and where the ball was headed. In my junior year of high school, I dropped out of the basketball team, as I knew I would never get to play very much, and went out for the "Golden Gloves" boxing tournament. Here I was pitted against young men of my own size, and we boxed under a very bright light, so I had *no* trouble seeing my opponent. Being in good shape, and having had my father teach me about boxing for years, I did very well.

I decided to lose weight in order to fight as a "lightweight" during my junior year, feeling I had a better chance to win at a lighter weight. I did win the lightweight championship of the Joplin Golden Gloves Regional Tournament around January of 1947. By 1948, I decided to box as a *wel-*

terweight, and was crowned welterweight champion that year. Although my father was sort of proud of me, Mother was embarrassed before her society friends—though she later found out that some of them even came to see me and enjoyed it. But both parents were afraid that I might turn out to be a pugilist and strongly discouraged my continuation in boxing. This was wise, because I have since realized that boxing is *very* damaging to the human body—if continued—and it was certainly better for me to do something other than try to beat somebody else's head in.

My body was, in fact, better suited for me to be a mile runner, and that is where I excelled the most. I won nearly all the mile runs in our various track meets in all three years of senior high school. The track coach of the University of Missouri, Tom Botts, ran up to me after my performance at the state track meet and offered me a partial *scholarship* to the University of Missouri if I would run on his track team. This was an honor, but God was calling me to His truth even then, and I had some things to think about before deciding which college to attend. World events were certainly moving along the way Mr. Armstrong had said they would, the Bible was making more and more sense to me, and I began to realize that I just *had* to go to Ambassador College someday to find out the *meaning* of life.

## Leadership Opportunities

As President of the Junior High Y Club and later as President of the Senior High Y Club, I was given a lot of opportunities to develop *leadership*. Still later, I was sent to the Branson, Missouri, YMCA Camp as a camp counselor, having eight little boys in my cabin to watch over and follow through the entire program each day, and then sleeping near them at night to be sure they were okay. But we were also boys; we would go to the ice cream parlor to try to flirt with the local girls, and thought we were having a "big night on the town." In my last year of high school, I was selected as a member of the National Honor Society. Later, I was elected President of the Junior College Luncheon Club. This club was devoted to studying and discussing world events and similar topics. Interestingly, it seemed to fit in very well with my desire to understand world events in relation to prophecy, which was beginning to develop.

After graduating from high school in May of 1948, my friend David Korn and I hitchhiked all the way to Hollywood, California. Hitchhiking was not illegal in those days. During the war and for a few years af-

# The Autobiography of Roderick C. Meredith

Pictured with Joplin High School track team (second row, far right)

ter they even had the slogan "Give a soldier a lift," as many servicemen were trying to go to and from their homes on weekends off the military base. So, David and I headed out to Hollywood thinking we could get exciting jobs as pageboys in a Hollywood motion picture studio. This idea came because David's father owned a photography studio and personally knew Robert Cummings—a fairly well-known Hollywood actor at that time. However, when we got to Hollywood, we found out that Mr. Cummings was off in Europe filming a movie on location over there. So, we had *no* help getting a job from him or anyone else.

Besides, at that time, *thousands* of employees of the motion picture industry were out of jobs and looking for other work. So, David and I had to make do by getting jobs as dishwashers and bus boys in restaurants. At first, I was the only one able to get a job, so I would sneak some food out of the restaurant to help David have enough to eat—with the kind connivance of my employer. And we found a nice lady over on a quiet street who ran a small restaurant where we would eat some warm chicken soup at night to give us some good nourishment. She sensed what was happening to us—it was quite obvious—and she loaded extra helpings of chicken into the soup to help us. I have been grateful for the help I have received from such wonderful ladies over the years.

We stayed at the Hollywood YMCA and were able to use its workout facilities at no charge, and we had a simply *wonderful* time wandering around Hollywood that summer of 1948. We were able to go to the famous "Muscle Beach" in Santa Monica on the streetcar for practically nothing, over to the Hollywood Bowl, and other places of interest. It was a wonderful and educational experience—even though we were virtually penniless. Yet, being young men, we really didn't worry about it too much and were *ashamed* to write home asking for money. After a few weeks, a couple of fellows who worked with us as bus boys in the Hollywood Athletic Club decided to go up to Oregon to work in the woods. I had always wanted to be a lumberjack and thought this would make me strong. So, the idea really appealed to me, and I suggested that they write us if it turned out okay up there. They said they would. After a few days, I realized we had only known them for about a week and decided that they would probably not bother to write—but they *did*. A day or two after that a letter arrived telling us to come up to Oakland, Oregon, and saying there was plenty of work up there. So, we went up on the Greyhound Bus, got jobs as lumberjacks for a couple of weeks, and had a good, masculine experience. However, my friend David came down with a serious case of poison oak and had to stop working in the woods. He ended up working for the Martin Box Company in town, and after a week or so, I joined him so we could be together.

Meanwhile, we were paying for room and board at the boarding house of Mr. and Mrs. W. D. Wilson there in Oakland. They were a kindly, middle-aged couple. After a week or so of mainly staying in our own room and going into their dining room for breakfast and dinner, I wandered into their living room. There, on the mantle over the fireplace, was a picture of Mr. and Mrs. Herbert W. Armstrong. This encouraged me—as I had continued hearing Mr. Armstrong on the radio and read Uncle Paul's copies of the *Plain Truth* magazine from time to time. I asked them about Mr. Armstrong, and they told me that he certainly "made sense" and that they had heard from others in that area that he was a man of great understanding. Again, I had been thinking more and more about Ambassador College and what to do. My grandmother had encouraged me to just stay in junior college for one year to "think it over" before heading out to Ambassador or to the University of Missouri. Looking back, I think she was thoughtful in this—and also giving in to her nurturing instinct to "keep Roderick close to home."

**Growing Up**

But I was strong and confident—and certainly would have gone out to Ambassador if I had known more about it at the time. Meanwhile, one evening, one of the other young men staying in our boarding house became very belligerent toward my friend David Korn. For *no* reason, it seemed, he began to push him around and threaten to beat him up. David was a kind and decent person in every way, and I was *infuriated* that this other young man would try to humiliate him. Even though the other fellow was somewhat older and taller than me, I jerked him through the hallway outside into the yard and told him we would settle things out there. As we began to fight, he quickly realized I knew more about fighting than he did and pulled a *knife* out from his pocket there under the streetlights, threatening me with that dangerous-looking weapon. That infuriated me even *more*, so I used one of my old *jujitsu* moves, grabbed and twisted his wrist—making him drop the knife—and proceeded to beat him badly. All the rest of the time we were there, this young man was very quiet and well behaved, and did not try to harass David or me anymore.

Yet I came to realize that this was *not* the true Christian thing to do. At that time, I did not really understand the full meaning of Christianity; I was simply trying to protect my friend. My athletic training and courage did come in handy on several occasions over the years, and I would *strongly* recommend to parents that they encourage their young boys to become strong and masculine so that they may, in similar emergencies, at least protect their mothers, wives, or girlfriends if necessary—*without* killing anybody.

Heading back to Joplin at the end of the summer, now in terrific shape and filled with confidence, I took a few days to help my friend Monty and his dad recondition an old building that they were going to turn into a store. We were sanding the old hardwood floor, and the sawdust had some type of resin or similar substance in it. We would put the sawdust into washtubs and take it to the city dump. As we were dumping the dust out of the third or fourth washtub, suddenly a breeze came up and a big flame flared right in my face. My eyebrows were singed, and I received burns on my nose and *serious* burns on my arms, as I had been holding the washtub down close to the fire. I was taken to a hospital and spent about eight days with my hands on pillows after being filled with too much penicillin, as my doctor admitted later.

For *months* afterward, my arms were weak, I felt somewhat dizzy and tired more than I had ever felt, and it became obvious that the serious burns and especially the administration of *far* too much penicillin had adversely affected my body. Looking back, I can see that God began to *humble* me through this and other similar situations so that I would be more willing and intent on truly seeking God and looking beyond the activities in junior college—sports, dating, and activities with my friends.

When I went out for the Golden Gloves in January 1949, I was immediately made aware that the skin on my arms was still tender, for in the very first sparring session, my skin literally started to *tear* off my arms and I was not able to continue. Then, for the first time in its history, the college *canceled* the track season that spring and had all the fellows go out for spring football, and I could not participate in that either.

**God Starts Dealing with Me**

What to *do*? Being energetic and always wanting to "get involved," I went out for drama and ended up having a part in a play about the life of Jesus Christ. Of all things, it seemed that God was pushing me in that direction in many ways that I cannot here fully describe.

Although I majored in Business Administration, I also took courses that year in both philosophy and psychology. Slowly I came to realize that all the reasonings of the so-called great thinkers of the world—Aristotle, Plato, and others—were empty ramblings that proved absolutely *nothing* about the real *meaning* of life that I had been seeking. I felt compelled to start reading the Bible more than ever and I heard Mr. Armstrong many evenings, writing for a subscription to *The Plain Truth* magazine and requesting a copy of his booklet *The United States and Britain in Prophecy*. All the literature from Mr. Armstrong *absolutely* made sense, made God much more real than anything else had, and began to impel me to go to Ambassador College that coming autumn to find out what life was all about.

However, that summer, *still* not having made up my mind for sure about where to go, I journeyed with a couple of friends out to Boise, Idaho, and obtained a job on the maintenance crew of a big government dam project at Anderson Ranch Dam, located about 70 miles northeast of Boise. It was an interesting and exciting summer, with much outdoors work and many fascinating experiences. My two friends and I lived in a kind of a military bunkhouse, and—with other young men—played penny poker into the night quite often, as we had nothing else to do.

About every other weekend, we would go down to Boise to see the sights. One of the older fellows there sensed how sincerely religious I was and, before leaving for Boise, would give me *half* of all his money to keep until Sunday morning. I asked him, "Why?" He, being very open and "macho," let me know that he was going to spend the first half on wine, women, and song. Not being as old or nearly as wild in that way, my two friends and I would wander around town looking into various bars and places of interest and perhaps having a beer or cup of coffee. But a couple of times we spotted this fellow hugging or dancing closely with a "B-girl" and getting ready for sex, for he had been in the military service and was, as religious people would say, "very carnal."

However, the next morning, he would ask me for the *other* half of the money he had given me for safekeeping. I asked him why he was doing this. He said, "Well, I do my own thing on Saturday nights, and I give the other half to the priest on Sunday morning, and that sort of takes care of things."

That got me thinking.

In *his* religion, you did whatever you wanted to do and then "confessed" to the priest the next day and gave him some money. Is the Creator of the universe "bought off" with that kind of behavior? This experience and many others helped me to think through *carefully* what true religion was all about. For example, a couple of Mormon boys on our maintenance crew with whom I was very friendly invited me down to Salt Lake City over the fourth of July weekend. Here, we had a good time together and I enjoyed their company. However, I quickly began to realize—going here and there throughout the city to various youth parties—that although these people did *not* indulge in drinking or smoking while in Salt Lake City, they certainly had *other* interests very heavily in mind. Getting back to the camp, I noticed that these fellows were sometimes smoking and drinking there at the workplace. I asked them about this. "You are not supposed to be drinking and smoking," I said, "and yet you do it up here. Why?" One of them answered, "Well, we know it's not the best, but up here we're sort of on *vacation*."

## Seeking Truth

Again, I had to *think*. Can you go "on vacation" from God? True religion—it became apparent to me—was something that ought to be *consistent*. And there ought to be a genuine willingness to obey the Creator *if* God is real and *if* the Bible really means what it says.

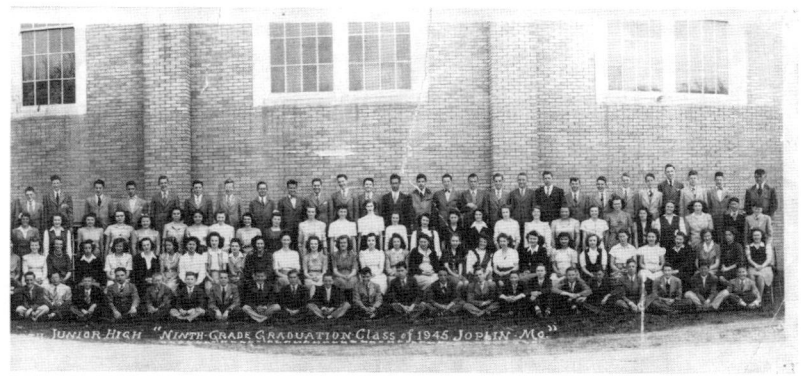

Grade 9 class photo, 1945 (back row, eleventh from left)

Pictured (#39) with junior high basketball team in 1943

At the Reserve Officers Training Corps Ball in 1948

# Chapter 3
## Embracing God's Calling

Through all these experiences, I continued to sincerely seek God. I learned to pray on my *knees* more than ever before and I read the Bible for *understanding* more than I had back in my Protestant church and at home. Yet, as I look back, I realize that Satan knew this and was trying to *block* me from going to Ambassador College and finding the absolute truth of Almighty God.

I had three nearly fatal experiences, which I began to realize were intended to wake me up and help me to find out the truth. The first of these was when my foreman parked our pick-up truck near the edge of the cliff overlooking the big dam we were building. He parked too close and somehow forgot to set the brake. So, after he got out, the pick-up began to slowly creep forward toward the edge of the cliff—heading toward *death* for me if I didn't do something. Instead of trying to save only myself, I jumped over into the driver's seat and pushed on the brake and pressed the emergency brake hard. After I got out, I looked and noticed that only two or three inches were between the front wheels of the pick-up and the edge of the cliff. I had tried to save the truck rather than saving myself alone—and God had mercy on me on that occasion.

A few days later, a fellow employee and I were walking along the edge of the cliff overlooking the spillway in the canyon below. A big dump truck swerved wildly toward us, and we had to literally *jump* out of the way—although we were already at the edge of the road and he should have given us some leeway. As we jumped, I again found myself looking *down* hundreds of feet into the canyon into which I could easily have fallen.

A few days after that, I and my friend from Joplin, Hal Richardson, were going fishing in the cold, rushing stream below the dam. Being more agile, I beat Hal to the edge of the ravine and began to adjust my fishing tackle—standing right next to the roaring river. Suddenly, Hal yelled at me, "*Look out!*"

As I quickly turned, a huge boulder zoomed right past me—barely grazing my forehead—and crashed into the river. I felt a tingling on my forehead. Pulling out my pocket handkerchief, I wiped off a few drops of blood. This huge boulder had come so *close* to my brain that it had scratched my forehead. I was *shaken,* for I realized that, *if* God had permitted it, this boulder could have come a half-inch closer to my brain and either killed me or knocked me into the roaring river where I would have drowned before any help could get to me.

I began to pray more fervently and sincerely cried *out* to God for understanding. As I did this and studied the Bible, it became clear to me that I simply had to prove to myself where God was working and what His purpose was for my life.

The summer ended a few weeks later, and I had determined to take the bus to Pasadena, California, and enroll at Ambassador College.

## Starting at God's College

I stayed in a small trailer house parked right next to my Uncle Paul's house. He and Aunt Ethel had moved out from Joplin to Pasadena. He had given up his veterinary practice to "serve God" and enrolled in Ambassador College. This began a key turning point in my life, for I was certainly experiencing my *own* "rendezvous with destiny." After a few weeks, I was able to get a room in the college dormitory called "Mayfair." It had been a large, high-class rooming house where older, wealthy women had lived. Mr. Armstrong was able to buy it with very little expenditure because it had become somewhat run down and some of the residents had died or moved out.

So, the only girl in college for the first three years, Betty Bates, lived *with* the "house mother," Annie Mann. She was a sparky Canadian woman, tough on the outside but very kind inside, and ideal to guide us young people along the right path. The college boys lived on the third floor of Mayfair—now absent all women. A few of the older

# Embracing God's Calling

Ambassador College roommate Herman Hoeh

outside roomers lived on the first and second floors, with Annie Mann and Betty living together on the first floor in a separate apartment.

Immediately, I was to become very well acquainted with all the early college students: Herman Hoeh, Raymond Cole, Kenneth Herrmann, Marion McNair, and Raymond McNair, plus the other young men who had come in that year with me, including Owen Smith, Paul Smith, and Gene Carter. Additionally, my uncle had his own home, and Mr. Armstrong's elder son, Richard David—also a student—lived at home with his parents.

It was a wonderful experience to get to know the early students and members of the tiny Church of God congregation meeting in the library of Ambassador College. They included Dr. Ralph Merrill, M.D.; Dr. and Mrs. Hal Lisman; Mr. and Mrs. Jack Elliott (later a college teacher); Mr. and Mrs. Eddie Eckhardt; Bill Homberger; Annie Mann; and many others. It seemed that *everyone* in this little group loved the others and was determined to learn more about the Bible—to *study* hard, to prove what the Bible actually said, and to try to live by it through the help of God's Spirit.

## Atmosphere of Ambassador College

At Sabbath services, Mr. Armstrong powerfully preached right out of the Bible—reading verse after verse and actually *explaining* and *expounding* those verses in detail. Virtually everyone brought his or her own Bible and were constantly encouraged by Mr. Armstrong to check up on him and prove what the Bible actually said. Afterward, if there were any questions, the brethren would come up and ask Mr. Armstrong, and he never rebuked them for this but tried to answer and prove to them the real *meaning* of the Bible in a way that was very clear and understandable.

The services lasted three full *hours* in those days. Later, when the services were cut back to two-and-a-half hours, some thought we were "becoming Laodicean." This kind of shows you in a humorous way how such things can affect people. But the sincere desire to learn the truth of the Bible and the *purpose* of human existence certainly permeated that little group of brethren and the atmosphere at Ambassador College. On Friday nights, we young men on the third floor of Mayfair would have regular "bull sessions" where we would discuss world news, current events, philosophical concepts, Bible prophecies, and related issues. It was fascinating and stimulating to me, and I *thank* God for it and the opportunity He gave me to be right in on the "ground floor" of the Work of God at that time.

Yet in the first letter I received from my mother, she enclosed an article from the old *Liberty* magazine, warning people about the various cults in California. She strongly urged me to be *sure* of what I was doing, to check up on Mr. Armstrong, and to not leave mainstream religion. So, I wrote her back that I was *very* independent—as she deeply knew—and would immediately leave Ambassador College if I found that it was a cult or that there was any kind of immorality or hypocrisy involved. She knew I meant it and never tried to press me on that again.

I, personally, did want to prove things to myself. So, I went around all over the campus asking *questions* about Mr. and Mrs. Armstrong, personally asking Esther Olsen—the elderly lady who received and counted the mail—*who* handled the money, *where* it was banked, *how* it was used, and all kinds of other related questions. Years later, Mr. Armstrong kidded me about my early attempt to check him out. He had heard about it, but he told me it was just fine, as "there was nothing to hide."

Years later, Mrs. Armstrong told me, "Rod, my husband could not be a hypocrite, for *everything* he thinks comes right out of his mouth." Over my 36 years of very close relationship with Mr. Armstrong, I came to realize that this was absolutely true, for Herbert W. Armstrong was truly a "big man"—and, like most other great leaders and individualists, he certainly made mistakes. He often freely admitted this. I am not talking about sin here, but about normal human foibles and missteps, which are common to all of us.

Interestingly to me at the time, I saw that Mr. Armstrong never tried to act religious or sound religious. He was very down to earth and practical, coming across as a dynamic businessman and leader rather than some theologian in an ivory tower. He had become sick of people playing politics in churches and acting religious while being hypocritical in the way they lived. Mr. Armstrong sincerely tried with all his heart to *find* the truth, *teach* the truth, and *live* the truth. He was not perfect, but I can sincerely say that I found in the thousands of hours I spent with him that he always tried and—in the end—succeeded more than most people I have ever known.

The truth—as I came to fully understand later—is not always what people think or imagine it should be, for the *real* truth, as Jesus Christ explained, is what the inspired word of God, the Holy Bible, actually *says*. That is *why* Jesus Christ said, "Your word is truth" (John 17:17) and "Man shall not live by bread alone, but by *every word of God*" (Luke 4:4). And again, "You shall know the truth, and the truth shall *make you free*" (John 8:32).

In fact, when I first began to attend the Church of God—meeting in the early years in the Ambassador College library—we seldom talked about "when we came into the Church." Rather, it was always "when I came into the truth," for, as we all began to realize, *genuine* Christianity is an *entire* way of life based upon the Bible, which is the truth. It should affect the way we speak, dress, eat, treat our fellow man, perform on the job or in our profession, involve ourselves in recreation and entertainment, etc. It involves trying to genuinely *honor* and *obey* our Creator. It involves a *total* surrender to let the real Jesus Christ of the Bible live *His* life within us through the Holy Spirit (Galatians 2:20). I have found that while *many* Protestants sometimes talk this way, extremely *few* actually surrender their entire lives to actually doing what the Bible clearly says. Most people water down the clear biblical teachings regarding lying, cheating, stealing, sexual practices, the days we observe for religious worship, etc.

My first few years at Ambassador College were quite a revelation, as I saw dozens—and, finally, *thousands*—of very sincere people attempting, with God's help, to actually live by the Bible. Our brethren regularly brought their Bibles and often their children to Sabbath services. With the straightforward, sincere, and powerful preaching of Herbert W. Armstrong, the Radio Church of God, as it was called then, began to grow steadily in size and in spiritual understanding. Again, Herbert Armstrong said regularly, "Don't just believe *me*, believe what you see right there in *your own Bible!*"

## Friendship with Dick Armstrong

During my years in college, Mr. Armstrong's older son, Dick, and I became good friends along with Herman Hoeh and Raymond McNair. So, I was able to go over to Mr. Armstrong's home and get acquainted with him and Mrs. Armstrong more fully than I would have otherwise done. I joined them at times for breakfast, eating "Armstrong Special"—otherwise known as *cornflakes*. Mrs. Armstrong's mother had died when she was a small child, so Mrs. Armstrong was not an expert at cooking and doing things along that line. And they had been poverty-stricken during the Great Depression in the early years of Mr. Armstrong's ministry—as he explains in his own autobiography. So, their diet was very simple for many years.

Seeing this and hearing Dick Armstrong, his mother, and others tell in graphic detail of the hardships they had gone through—and Mr. Armstrong's *total* commitment to do the Work of God no matter what—inspired me to go "all out" when God finally called me to full understanding and placed me in His ministry. Mrs. Armstrong became like a "second mother" to many of us students. We enjoyed getting her advice and motherly perspective.

Mr. Armstrong had to be a "fighter," because—for the first few years—he was the *only* converted member of the faculty at Ambassador College. I well remember our old French teacher and others talking about "when this thing folds up." I also tried to "rescue" Betty Bates from this teacher's wrath one time in class, for this carnal old professor was arrogantly belittling Mr. Armstrong and describing him as "the heavenly father" and Dick Armstrong as the "son of God with his red chariot" (Dick did own a small Plymouth convertible, as he worked long hours dubbing the radio broadcast discs that were sent out to the stations all over the world). Betty tried to defend Mr. Armstrong in class from this arrogant professor. Being somewhat of a fighter myself, I stood up in class and told this old fellow to "leave Betty alone" and to stop criticizing Mr. Armstrong.

Blazing with anger, the professor turned on me and threatened to "take me to Mr. Armstrong" right then. I told him, in effect, "That's great. Let's go right *now*."

Realizing what he might be getting into, the upset professor ordered me out of the class. So, I went alone to Mr. Armstrong and explained the situation. He chuckled and told me it would be all right and that he would handle the situation when the professor had simmered down. Mr. Armstrong had to be *very* patient in those early years with a lot of carnal and even sometimes *hostile* professors who certainly did not agree with the spiritual foundation of Ambassador College. At the end of the semester, I got a "B-" in that French course, but I hated to bother Mr. Armstrong with what I knew was a very small matter and I let it stand, though I felt I had earned a better grade.

## The Feast of Tabernacles

Each autumn, the local brethren and the entire student body would head off for several days to attend one of the biblical Festivals called the "Feast of Tabernacles" (Zechariah 14:16–19; John 7:1–14). In those early years this Festival was held at Belknap Springs, Oregon, about 70 miles east of Eugene in the beautiful Cascade Mountains.

Being so new to the truth, it was a truly exciting and eye-opening time to me, for Mr. Armstrong—now in his late 50s—gave very informative and inspiring sermons and Bible studies for eight days in a *row*. The brethren brought their Bibles to each service to thoroughly check out what was being said, and they put dozens of questions to Mr. Armstrong about *anything* they disagreed with or didn't understand. But it all came back to what the Bible actually *says,* and I was constantly impressed with the depth of Mr. Armstrong's biblical knowledge and his willingness to share that understanding in a patient, thorough, and unthreatening way; he had the truth, and even all by itself, the truth is *powerful.*

After my first year at Ambassador College, Kenneth Herrmann, Owen Smith, and I drove up to Oregon to work in the woods and replenish our financial resources. Finding that we would be staying at least part-time at the home of Mr. and Mrs. David Henion, Sr., Mr. Armstrong advised us that it would be okay to attend Sabbath services at the local Seventh-Day church of God right there in Jefferson, Oregon. He had known many of those people and told us, "I originally started that church and they have retained most of the truth. So, go ahead and attend with them, as it is too far to drive to where we now have churches." Then Mr. Armstrong said with a chuckle, "Those good country people can't mislead you. But you might worry them or some of their leaders."

And, indeed, we did—when Ken, Owen, and I first walked into services on the Sabbath, the lead minister looked very worried when he found out we were from Ambassador College. As I later learned, he was afraid that "Armstrong's men" had come to take over. But we were not "Armstrong's men." We were college kids in our early 20s and had just come there to worship God on His Sabbath day. Later, the minister and his flock came to realize this and were all very friendly and cordial to us from then on.

One week, after Sabbath services, we were invited to have lunch at the Henions' along with A. F. Dugger—the brother of Andrew Dugger—who was for a time the leading minister of the Church of God (Seventh Day). It was helpful for me to "take his measure" so to speak, and to realize that this man, though perhaps sincere, did not in any way reflect the capacity, the knowledge, or the vision of reaching out to "all the nations" that Mr. Armstrong had.

We young men, now "lumberjacks," worked long, hard hours felling and bucking timber. We slept most of the summer in tents or cleaned-out chicken houses. We took turns bathing in one of the old tubs our bosses had brought along. And we were blessed that they were Sabbath-keepers—we came bumping down from the mountains in our jeep every Friday evening and were able to get a warm shower at the Henions' home. How good a warm shower felt and how good it was to sleep in a regular bed each Friday and Saturday night.

**Made Student Body President**

During the last half of my third year in college, I was made Student Body President and spent even more time with Mr. Armstrong. Also, I began to help Herman Hoeh get out the *Good News* magazine and later *The Plain Truth*. These regularly scheduled magazines—coming out steadily for the first time *ever*—contributed to the steady growth in attendance and financial stability of the entire Work.

After my third year of college, Mr. Armstrong sent Raymond McNair and me on a baptizing tour all over the United States. We were not sent out to try to "convert" people, as some might suppose. Rather, we were visiting those who had already *requested* baptism—some of them had waited for years for someone from the Church to be able to visit them and talk to them about baptism and the whole purpose of life. Meeting these sincere people throughout the entire

South and Midwest of the United States not only helped them, but changed my *life*, for I could see how God was really bringing these people to a *dedicated* life of actually obeying God and *doing* what the Bible says. At the end of our visit, they would sometimes break down and cry, knowing that they might never again meet anyone from Ambassador College or anyone who knew the truth, for, at that time, the Radio Church of God only had *three* congregations—one in Pasadena, California; one in Eugene, Oregon; and one in Portland, Oregon. There were no congregations and *no* ministers east of the Rockies.

As we went through the South, we were sometimes accosted by the old-fashioned Southern sheriffs—especially if we were counseling or baptizing any of our black brethren. They would threaten us by their approach and ask, "Are the two of you civil rights workers, here to cause trouble?" And we would let them know that we were simply ministerial students sent out to baptize people and then leave them to work out their own salvation. We told them that we were *not* involved in politics.

With Ambassador College classmates (left to right) Herman Hoeh, C. Paul Meredith, and Norman Smith in front of C.D. Meredith's home in July 1953

Conducting a baptism at the Feast of Tabernacles in Seigler Springs, 1952

# Chapter 4
## Early Ministry

I will *always* remember the country lady from Kansas who met with us along the way with her friend. She had brought this Protestant friend as a companion when she was meeting "these young men from California." At the end of our visit, after we had counseled, baptized, and laid hands on her for her to receive the Holy Spirit (Acts 8:17), she asked us to notice something. And I hasten to add that we were through with our visit and she had nothing to gain by bringing this up. She was obviously not "Pentecostal" or overly emotional, but very normal and steady—as was her lifelong Protestant friend. She told us how she had sent off for an anointed cloth from Mr. Armstrong the previous winter because one of her arms had never developed properly and was only about a fourth as large as the other. The smaller arm had simply hung limp "like a rope," she said. After receiving the anointed cloth (Acts 19:11–12), her crippled arm had been growing "right back" steadily.

Then she held out her arms—it was summertime and she was wearing a short-sleeved dress. She showed us how both arms were about the same, but the one that had been healed was a tiny bit smaller. She said, with feeling, "God *healed* this arm supernaturally. But He is letting *me* milk the cows with both hands and develop the muscles in the arm by myself." Somehow, the way she said that with great sincerity brought tears to my eyes. God *is* the Healer. But He does not heal nearly as often as He did in Christ's time, for as Jesus said, "When the Son of Man comes, will He really find faith on the earth?" (Luke 18:8).

Though Mr. Armstrong had told us young men not to overdo it, lose sleep, or harm ourselves in any way, we were extremely zealous—absolutely *determined* to reach all the people we could during these summer tours. So, we often missed meals, lost sleep, and did without in many ways. Yet there was a tremendous sense of fulfillment. We knew that we were, in fact, walking with God, as we saw so many things working out for us—often in remarkable ways. We saw no movies, had *no* dates with pretty girls, and had almost no kind of normal fun as most young people would expect. Though we were only in our early 20s, we had really come to *know* the Bible. So, we were able to thoroughly rebut Protestant ministers who were sometimes invited out with these people to witness their baptisms. These ministers would try to ask us trick questions about the Sabbath or other matters, and we were able to go right down the line through the Bible and thoroughly refute them. They were often astonished that such young men knew the Bible so much better than they did.

At the end of the summer's baptizing tour of 1951 with Raymond McNair, he and I drove night and day from Oklahoma City so we could arrive in time for the student orientation of the fall semester at Ambassador College in Pasadena. I had already been appointed Student Body President—having replaced Raymond Cole the previous February, who'd had to drop out of college for a few months because of serious illness. So, I finished the last third of my junior year as Student Body President, and now continued in that responsibility for my entire senior year. That threw me into very close contact with Mr. Armstrong—although I'd already had a fairly close relationship with him and Mrs. Armstrong because of my friendship with Dick Armstrong. Dick and I had spent many evenings taking the old *World Tomorrow* radio program discs out to the airport and hanging out together on many occasions, and we were very good friends.

**Started Building "The Work"**
Now, as Student Body President, I needed to go to Mr. Armstrong regularly and talk over student affairs. He appeared to relish this, as his son Ted was off in the Navy and Dick did not spend a lot of time with his dad in the same ways Ted had. Mr. Armstrong and I became genuinely good *friends*—and shared *hundreds* of occasions together. Mrs. Armstrong became like a "second mother" to me and many other stu-

## Early Ministry

dents during those early years in Ambassador College. By now, I was very deeply committed to the Church and realized how important it was for the Work to be carried out, and I felt that Herman Hoeh, Raymond McNair, and I, among others, would simply help Mr. Armstrong do the Work whether we were ordained or not. In fact, it did not even *occur* to me, strange as it may sound, that I would become a minister or become ordained. I had always felt that real ministers were older—like Dr. Ridpath, the Methodist minister of my childhood, and like Mr. Armstrong himself. I simply wanted to help do the Work.

But during my senior year I helped Mr. Armstrong think through many situations and began to work with him on a more intimate basis than ever before. Also, Herman Hoeh and I had *already* managed to get *The Good News* magazine coming out regularly. And by halfway through the following year, we began to get out *The Plain Truth* as well. The Editorial Office for the entire Work of God—except for Mr. Armstrong's personal office—was in the Mayfair basement, below where the students lived.

We had an old rickety card table there with an old stand-up lamp, and Herman Hoeh and I would write articles there and talk over things regarding the magazines between our classes and at night. Elva Russell—later Mrs. Richard Sedliacik—was now a sophomore student and was *extremely* helpful acting as our secretary. She would type our articles after they had been scribbled out or dictated, and she was willing to get up at 3:00 a.m.—or *any* time—to help us meet Editorial deadlines. She was a remarkable person and a wonderful help. Incidentally, she was a faithful and zealous member of the Living Church of God until her death, and she actually helped me put together some information to fill in details of this very autobiography.

After my graduation from Ambassador College in early June 1952, I led a nationwide baptizing tour with Burk McNair over the entire United States and on into Canada. We were gone eleven full weeks and traveled over 19,000 miles during that time. We spent *hundreds* of hours driving, counseling, talking, and strengthening the people on the tour, again losing meals and sleep the entire time, as we were very dedicated young men in a fast-growing Work. We *did* get some persecution occasionally. I remember one farmer, whose wife had requested a visit, pointing a gun at us and threatening us with what he would do if we did not immediately leave without visiting with her. Another man, in Tacoma, Washington, called

41

up and tried to threaten me during the night. I hated to wake Burk up as one of us had to be awake the next day, so I went out and talked to this man and his wife at their home—which could have been very dangerous. But we were young, vigorous, and had very little fear in those days. Youthful bravery, I suppose—yet we did have a great deal of faith in God as well.

**God Always Cared for Us**

As Burk and I drove across the United States, we literally went by faith, as we were many times virtually without money. We were driving an old Chrysler, which used a lot of gas, and we did need places to sleep and food to eat. So, we hoped that God would give us money as we went along, since the Business Manager, Vern Mattson, was unable to send us funds regularly. Mr. Armstrong always managed to use *all* the money available on radio stations and otherwise building the Work. One day, we were *completely* out of money, not knowing where we would sleep that night or what we would eat. At the end of the afternoon—after visiting with another party or two earlier—we visited a middle-aged lady and her elderly mother in a fairly large home out in a country area. It was in Kentucky, I believe.

After visiting them, counseling them, and baptizing them—just as we were about to leave—the younger woman said, "Wait a minute, fellows." Then she turned to her mother and said, "Mother, remember what we were going to give the boys?" My heart began to race a little bit as I realized that God might be helping us not to have to sleep in the car as we sometimes had to do, or to miss out on eating anything but dates, prunes, nuts, and other basics we kept in the car. The two women found an envelope they had waiting for us and gave it to us. It turned out to be about $55, as I remember. *Boy,* were we glad, for $55 in 1952 would equal about $500 in today's money.

So, we had enough money for food, gas, and motels for another few days. Because of these dear ladies and their willingness to save their tithes and offerings and give to these young men who were baptizing them on Mr. Armstrong's behalf—of course, in the name and service of Jesus Christ—our hearts were thankful to God that night.

In many such ways, we learned on those baptizing tours to live by faith, for often, at the last minute, God would intervene and take care of our basic needs. As long as we put Him first, He never failed to take care of us.

## Early Ministry

At the end of the summer, I asked Mr. Armstrong's permission to raise up a local congregation in San Diego, California, for Burk and I had baptized several people down there and had learned that there were a few others who had already been baptized. Remember, the only local congregations the Work had in those days were in Portland and Eugene, Oregon, and Pasadena, California—only three when I came to college, and still only three when I graduated.

So, I had the honor of establishing the first congregation raised up as a *result* of Ambassador College graduates in action. I went down and visited some of the people we had already counseled for baptism and found other members on the mailing list. Then, we met in "Dartlee Hall" just off Sixth Avenue in San Diego—right across from Balboa Park. It was a little, framed "Woman's Club" type of building with a nice lady who often sat in and heard our sermons—though she didn't understand what we were saying, as God was not calling her. But she was friendly and often made a kind remark about the "fine talk" we young men made in our sermons.

For that first service, I brought down four students from the college. One of the young men gave the sermonette and one of the girls played the piano. We had *seven* "locals" who turned up for that first service—making a total of exactly *twelve* people for the first service in San Diego. We did not plan it that way, but I feel it was significant, as twelve is the number of "organizational beginnings," as Mr. Armstrong explained many times. Most of you know that the Bible records twelve patriarchs, twelve tribes of Israel, twelve Apostles, twelve gates into the Holy City, etc.

Thinking back, I wonder how a 22-year-old man like me could even begin to *do* that. We could because we had been given a great deal of thorough training from Mr. Armstrong and were extremely dedicated and sincere. We were Depression and World War II babies and had grown up in a time of stress, learning the need for dedication in both national emergencies.

Also, since the Radio Church of God was just beginning to expand, the messages we had for these people were *exciting* and *new*, for there were only four or five booklets and there was no correspondence course. Therefore, even though we were young, we were able to be their leaders, since we certainly did know more than they did, and they could see and appreciate that, despite our youth.

By the time we had the second or third Sabbath service in San Diego, I had invited Mr. Harold Jackson—later our first black evangelist—to come to Sabbath services, for Burk McNair and I had baptized his wife on the tour that summer, but they were not yet sure they would be accepted by the white brethren in the Church. You younger readers may need to be reminded that in 1952, many parts of America were still at least partially segregated. But after the first one or two Sabbaths, it became obvious that—in the more open-minded atmosphere in San Diego—it would be just fine for them to attend. So, they were glad to attend and, after asking my permission, Mr. Jackson brought his daughter, Theresa, along with her husband and child, to Sabbath services as well. So, we soon had five black brethren in the small-but-growing San Diego congregation, and I had the honor and privilege of bringing the first black people into the Radio Church of God.

**In the Field**

At the Feast of Tabernacles in 1953, we had a wonderful Feast—and a startling announcement from Herman Hoeh, for Mr. Hoeh (not yet Dr.) got up for a sermon and began to describe how Mr. Armstrong was not a prophet, as some had supposed. I noticed Mr. Armstrong *bolt* upright from his seat. I wondered if he was going to go on stage and throw Mr. Hoeh off. But he listened as Mr. Hoeh carefully explained that Mr. Armstrong was doing the overall work of building an entire *era* of the Church of God and was, therefore, an apostle. That was startling to all of us—including Mr. Armstrong. So, although Mr. Armstrong did not correct Mr. Hoeh during the sermon, he did stride vigorously toward the stage right after Mr. Hoeh finished and said, "Brethren, Mr. Hoeh startled me in what he was saying today. I had in no way talked to him about this and am still trying to think it over. I am not absolutely sure he is correct. But as I think about the fruits of what Christ has done, I realize he may be correct. So, let's all think and pray about this. However, don't any of you go around calling me an apostle, as outsiders may think we are crazy."

Interestingly, Mr. Armstrong *seldom* referred to himself as an apostle, or as having the apostolic rank or its authority, until some ministers began to turn on him from time to time in later years—including his own son Ted. Then, he felt the need to let people know who he was and the *position* that Jesus Christ had given him in God's

## Early Ministry

Church. I always admired his humility on this and learned from that example.

### My First Field Pastorate

After the Feast, as I had been directed by Mr. Armstrong, I drove to Portland, Oregon, to be the "acting" pastor of the congregation there. Basil Wolverton, an older local elder, had pastored those brethren for years. They'd had to do without a regular, full-time pastor, as Basil was busy in his work as a professional cartoonist. Many of our older brethren will remember that Basil drew the pictures for the children's book *The Bible Story*. He was a very interesting character with a loving personality. It was good to have him helping me while I was there, since he had been around for so long and was so balanced.

Knowing I was lonesome and all alone, Basil and his wife Honor invited me about once a week to have a steak dinner at their home. On coming to the front door, Basil pushed a bottle of wine in my face and said, "You'll really like this." The label said, "Old Tennis Shoe." Of course, it was a "funny label"—and Basil was full of funny sayings and tricks all through the evening. So, he made the time there interesting and enjoyable—and I have always appreciated the help, warmth, and friendship of Basil and Honor Wolverton. Chloe Schippert, one of the local deaconesses in the Portland congregation, wrote me encouraging notes almost every week after I would preach. She would tell me what a wonderful or helpful sermon I had given. Of course, I was smart enough to realize that she was an older lady simply encouraging me. Yet it was still encouraging to have her respect and help each week in this way. She helped me in many other ways, and I have used her as an outstanding example of service in sermons throughout the years.

During this time, I was able to become acquainted with and help Mr. and Mrs. Leroy Neff, who would go on to do much service in the wider Church but were just local members of the Portland congregation at that time. Mrs. Neff had not yet been baptized, so I had the honor of baptizing her in the winter of 1952–53 during my pastorate in Portland. They have been my friends ever since.

About December 18, 1952, I was summoned to Pasadena to be ordained as an *evangelist* in the Church of God. I sincerely did not feel worthy of this, and even *argued* with Mr. Armstrong about it, for I did not know that he was an apostle at that time, and neither did he.

Nevertheless, he explained to me that I had been *doing* the job of a minister for several months since my graduation—leading a nationwide baptizing tour, raising up the congregation in San Diego, teaching Bible classes, writing articles, and now planning to raise up a new congregation in the Seattle/Tacoma area. So, after counseling with my uncle and with Herman Hoeh, I acquiesced—feeling that it was Christ who would guide this for good. Therefore, on December 20, 1952, I was one of the five *original* evangelists ordained by Herbert W. Armstrong in this era of the Work.

The ordination ceremony took place in front of the Church of God congregation meeting in the library of the College. First, Mr. Armstrong laid hands on Herman L. Hoeh, the first male student graduate of the college. Then they, in turn, laid hands on Raymond Cole, an older student who had grown up in the "Sardis Church"— Church of God (Seventh Day). Next, they all laid hands on Richard David Armstrong, Mr. Armstrong's oldest son. Then, they all laid hands on my uncle, Dr. C. Paul Meredith. Least, and fittingly last, for I was the youngest and the newest, they all laid hands on me and ordained me as an evangelist in the Church of God. It was a momentous occasion in my life, and one for which I have always been grateful. Now, as of this writing, I am the *only* one of those first evangelists still left alive.

My father—who was not a member of the Church but was supportive of me—wrote to congratulate me of this "signal honor," as he put it. Although feeling that I wasn't really ready, I returned to Portland to do my best as the local pastor there. Soon, I raised up another congregation in the Pacific Northwest in Tacoma—where the Seattle and Tacoma area brethren could meet together. Then, that spring, I was brought back down to Pasadena to assist Mr. Armstrong and the Dean of Students, and I began to take over some of the Theology classes in Ambassador College. That coming autumn, 1953, Herman L. Hoeh and I were given responsibility for all the theology courses—though Mr. Armstrong would come in from time to time as a guest lecturer.

Also, I began writing articles regularly for *The Good News* and later for *The Plain Truth*, as well as assisting in the Work in many other ways. My life had indeed been *dramatically* changed from the youthful years I had spent in Joplin, Missouri.

# Chapter 5
## Priceless Opportunities

About March or early April, Mr. Armstrong asked me to return to Pasadena to help him "settle down" the student body. They were having trouble because of a self-proclaimed "prophet" type of young man who had already caused a few notable people to become very disoriented in their spiritual walk and faith in Christ's leadership. So, I drove back down to Pasadena from Portland and was given a title never heard of before or since: "Graduate Assistant to the Dean of Students." Since I had just been the Student Body President during my senior year, I knew the students well and was able to confront the confusion sown by this very arrogant young man. After a week or two, Mr. Armstrong also gave me the wonderful responsibility of teaching the Freshman Bible Class for the last few weeks during the spring of 1953.

Interestingly, I had in that class Mr. Armstrong's youngest son, Garner Ted Armstrong, and other men who were later leaders in the Work. So, it was an eventful spring—especially since I was also able to begin attending the Graduate School classes under Mr. Armstrong. These Graduate School classes were conducted in a seminar fashion, with a great deal of conversation and give-and-take among five or six of us graduates and older students and Mr. Armstrong himself.

It was during this time that Mr. Armstrong first conceived of and introduced one of the most magnificent truths the Church of God has ever known. He started out by saying, "Fellows, I don't want to be a heretic. But it seems that God is putting in my mind something about what we will really be in the future beyond what we have ever known."

In the past, I vividly remembered how Mr. Armstrong always said that when we are "born again" and in God's Kingdom, we will be "like super-archangels." Any older brethren will remember that Mr. Armstrong didn't usually say "like" anything. He was usually very dogmatic and spoke with *authority*—as Jesus did. But he could sense that there was something *beyond* us being archangels. Yet, in the earlier years, he simply did not know what it was. So, during the spring of 1953, God began to reveal to him that as God made every creature "after its kind," so our Creator made man, also, after His kind—the God kind.

Genesis 1:26 tells us that "God said, 'Let Us make man in Our image, according to Our likeness; let them have dominion over the fish of the sea, over the birds of the air, and over the cattle, over all the earth and over every creeping thing that creeps on the earth.'" So, as God made each "beast of the earth *according to its kind*" (v. 25), He made mankind after His *own* kind—destined to be *full* members of the Family of God. If any of you reading this do not understand, please feel free to write our offices or call us and request the most thoroughly thought out and powerful booklet on this subject ever written. It is entitled *Your Ultimate Destiny*. [Editor's Note: This booklet has since been retitled *What Is the Meaning of Life?*] It will open your eyes to one of the most powerful and meaningful truths you have ever encountered, helping you understand what others in this world are unable to grasp—the real meaning of life itself.

I have always been grateful to have been in on the "ground floor"—as my uncle C. Paul Meredith reminded me—in actually having the privilege of being *there* when Mr. Armstrong introduced this and many basic points of truth during the early years of Ambassador College. Although Mr. Armstrong was very human and made human mistakes, he was deeply *committed* to learning and to understanding the real truth of the Bible and teaching others that truth and way of life.

Importantly, I should add for those who may be confused that Mr. Armstrong did not get *any* of this from the Mormon idea of "becoming gods" after this life. The teachings of the "Latter-Day Saints"—including non-biblical ideas like a pre-mortal existence, baptism for those already dead, and three different "kingdoms" with different levels of glory—are totally different from what God's word teaches and were arrived at from a totally different point of view. If you read literature about this, you will understand. Although Latter-Day Saints are often kind people and often have excellent family values, they certainly do not understand what the Bible actually says in *many* areas of teaching and practice.

## Continuing to Build the Work

After teaching the Freshman Bible Class and helping with student affairs during the last few weeks of the spring of 1953, I was then given the opportunity to lead Herman Hoeh on a baptizing tour across the southern states for the first half of the summer. Though Herman was my senior in academic and editorial ways, I was his senior in conducting these tours, in counseling people, and in understanding "average" people in many ways—as Herman was always very "academic." After conducting this tour for several weeks, I then flew back to Pasadena to take over the job of managing and getting out *The Plain Truth* and *The Good News* magazines, as Mr. Hoeh had to continue through the rest of the summer on the baptizing tour, with Norman Smith joining him.

During the fall of 1953, I was given a full teaching load—having started, with Mr. Armstrong's permission, the Epistles of Paul class, which we had never had before. Also, I continued to edit the magazines, pastor the San Diego congregation on weekends, and help Mr. Armstrong generally "manage" many aspects of the Work even in those years.

At the beginning of the summer of 1954, I had one of the most fascinating and eye-opening experiences of my entire life. I was given the opportunity to join Dick Armstrong on a three-and-a-half-month trip to Britain and Europe—returning with Mr. and Mrs. Armstrong just before the Day of Atonement that autumn. God certainly blessed us, as Mr. Armstrong sent us over *first class* on the largest and perhaps greatest steam ship of that kind, the original *Queen Elizabeth*.

We were pampered during the entire trip in many ways. We were even able to have gourmet meals at our assigned table with very successful men and women for five solid days. That was part of Mr. Armstrong's idea of "training" us as future leaders in the Work. I wrote to my parents soon after the ship landed at Southampton:

*June 21, 1954*
*Cumberland Hotel,*
*Marble Arch,*
*London, W.I.*

*Dear Folks:*

*This has been a most eventful day in my life—as have all the days for this past couple of weeks. It is good to be on land again, and to be writing you from England.*

*We also saw France this morning, as our ship anchored briefly in Cherbourg to let off passengers.*

*Our entire voyage across has been one of the most interesting and exciting experiences I could hope for. Going over first class on the world's largest and, I think, the finest ocean liner, is an incomparable treat. I wish that I could take time to relate in detail all the fascinating experiences I had coming over.*

*Briefly, let me say that we were treated like kings all the way. There were free concerts, movies, dances, and other entertainment to make every moment exciting, and, under the circumstances, very profitable.*

*All meals are included in the price of the ticket, and the first-class dining hall and menu were comparable to that of the finest restaurants in the world. We could have caviar every noon, steak every night, and practically anything we could think to order, whether it was on the menu or not. Wow! I am not sure, but I must have gained at least three or four pounds.*

*Our stewards helped us in every way possible to be comfortable, and we could have breakfast in bed, and lunch, or all the time. The rooms and furnishings on the Queen Elizabeth are certainly worthy of royalty, and indeed there are often some on the boat. A trip of this sort enables one to meet and chat with people you would seldom encounter in ordinary life, and I did get to know some very interesting people. Being all together in the midst of the sea seems to loosen people's inhibitions, and they are much more friendly and open than you would find*

# Priceless Opportunities

them under other circumstances. For instance, I got to know a Mr. Gordon, who is president of E.B. Roes Co., Ltd., of Canada. It is the largest aircraft manufacturer in Canada, so I suppose he is a millionaire. But I just happened to hit it off right with him in conversation, and I learned a lot from being with him.

Also, I had a lot of fun meeting a lot of the college students and grads who were on tours. The younger set kept things moving on the boat, and everyone had quite a gay time.

Maybe I should have taken more time to write, to study, and to sleep, but I felt it was a most rare experience, so I didn't want to miss a moment of it during the short five days. Anyway, I shall always remember it, and am rather glad I spent the time the way I did.

Dick and I were assigned to a dinner table with three other charming people, and I shall send you a photograph of our group (minus one), in the dining room. You get quite well acquainted with those at your table, and we all had a delightful time together.

England looked very pretty when we first saw it this afternoon, and I think that I shall like it here. Dick and I were met at the Southampton Pier by Bill and John Cousins, the brothers of one of the ladies in our Pasadena church. They took Dick right in as part of the family when he was last here, and it is good to have someone like that here. They met us with their car and brought our Hillman Minx so we would have plenty of luggage space.

Coming into London, we stopped for tea at "tea-time", and I began to realize that I am in a _different_ environment than I have ever known before. I think I shall like London.

We will be here at the Cumberland Hotel, but write me in c/o American Express, 6 Haymarket, London, W.I. England. My thoughts are with you.

Love,<br>Rod

Dick and I stayed at the Cumberland Hotel in London—located at the top of Park Lane near Marble Arch. We were only there a few weeks before leaving for the continent in Dick Armstrong's small Hillman Minx automobile. We drove all through Europe for five weeks and it was an extremely educational and eye-opening experience—to say the least. After we had returned to Britain for a couple of weeks, Mr. and Mrs. Armstrong arrived. They stayed at the Dorchester Hotel—an extremely fine hotel where we joined them most evenings. At the Dorchester, we always had to "dress" for dinner, meaning we wore our tuxedos at dinner—as we had also had to do, incidentally, *every* night on the *Queen Elizabeth*.

Then, Dick and I joined Mr. and Mrs. Armstrong in the public evangelistic meetings he conducted for our radio listeners in Belfast, Northern Ireland; in Glasgow, Scotland; and in London, England. We were somewhat surprised in Belfast to be met with an audience of about 700 people. This was almost the same number we had at the Feast of Tabernacles in America. But the people turned out in great numbers because they had heard Mr. Armstrong regularly on radio Luxembourg, and many were strongly anti-Catholic and *assumed* Mr. Armstrong was a Protestant minister whom they could support.

## Mr. Armstrong's Powerful Warning

When Mr. Armstrong spoke, he raised the hair on the back of European listeners' necks, for he *powerfully* predicted that, unless the British peoples truly turned to *God*, they would be brought *down* in a terrible coming tribulation and punishment for their turning away from the God of the Bible. And, even more than in most of his sermons in Pasadena, Mr. Armstrong was *specific*. He showed that the British Empire *would* come down. He showed that the great "sea gates"—such as the Suez Canal; control of the Cape of Good Hope around South Africa, Singapore, and the Malacca Straits; the Panama Canal; and the other great "gates" that God had promised the sons of Joseph—*would* be taken away unless we repented.

Specifically, Mr. Armstrong also showed that, although Germany was even then lying prostrate after total defeat in World War II, it would rise and become the dominant nation in a coming United States of Europe. In the early 1950s, and especially during these campaigns, I heard him say these things in person, and he was very *specific* and very powerful. I will *never* forget it.

# Priceless Opportunities

Back in London after the campaigns, Dick and I shared the same hotel suite with Mr. and Mrs. Armstrong in the Dorchester Hotel. It was a corner suite with a parlor in the corner, Mr. and Mrs. Armstrong's room on the left side, and a room for Dick and me on the other side. So, we had many close visits—the four of us often having breakfast together in our dressing robes. The Armstrongs treated me as another son during that time—Mrs. Armstrong was solicitous of my tie being straight and other things, as she might have been with her own sons. I enjoyed this warm, loving relationship with them on this trip and on many, many other occasions through the early years.

Near the end of the summer of 1954, Mr. and Mrs. Armstrong, Dick, and I flew together to visit Rome, Italy. It was the first visit to Rome for any of us and was truly eye-opening and educational in many respects. We got to see so many of the remarkable historical sites of Rome, including the caves along the Appian Way, where Christians were supposed to have met in secret in the earlier years of Christianity. We saw the absolutely magnificent wealth and splendor of Saint Peter's Basilica—built with the sweat and blood of tens of thousands of Europeans. The building of Saint Peter's indirectly helped precipitate the Reformation, for a man named Tetzel was sent around Europe by the Vatican collecting money to build Saint Peter's and—under the authority of the Roman Catholic Church—passing out "indulgences" to wealthy donors. Because these people were giving a lot of money to the church, they were considered able to sin and yet have their sins "forgiven" and get out of purgatory *much* sooner. Martin Luther and other Protestant leaders found the Roman Catholic Church doing several of these things and—over the years—all these things and more precipitated the massive Protestant Reformation that swept over Europe during the 1500s.

During our visit to Rome, Dick and I—separate from Mr. and Mrs. Armstrong—drove south into the Alban Hills to visit Castel Gandolfo, the Pope's summer residence. Here, inside a very large courtyard, the Pope appeared on his balcony before thousands of yelling, screaming, sweating, and even palpitating worshipers. Peasant women were shaking and crying as they waited for their "god" to appear on that balcony. And when he did appear, there was a scream of exaltation like God Himself had descended into the midst of the courtyard. I have never seen anything like it. Many human beings seem to need to worship a man—since the real God, the Creator, is invisible, and most people do not really know God or understand His written word, the Bible.

After returning from Rome, we returned to the United States with the Armstrongs on the *SS America*—once again going "first class." It was a wonderful experience to be with the Armstrongs and have this priceless opportunity. On the way back, the ship had a table tennis tournament going on and, as it turned out, I was able to win the prize for this table tennis championship. My prize? An *ashtray*. Of course, since I do not smoke, I kept it only as a souvenir, but it was fun being able to win the tournament, since Raymond McNair and I used to play table tennis for many hours together and even with Mr. Herbert Armstrong personally when he would come over to Mayfair to "warm up" before doing the radio broadcast and at many other times.

Now back in Pasadena, I found that Raymond's younger sister, Margie, had entered college. I was *very* interested in that fact, though I thought she was "too young" for me to date since she was only a freshman. Yet, before the end of the first year and into the second year of Ambassador College, both Dick Armstrong and George Meeker, and others who later became ministers, began to date Margie. That got me *very* concerned. So, I began to date her also and then stopped for a while—feeling she was "George Meeker's girl." We had a sort of "code of honor" among the students not to cut in on another man's girlfriend. But George took off for England on a trip similar to the one I had taken with Dick the previous summer, and I found that he had stopped writing or contacting Margie—so, it was time for me to move in.

During the summer of 1955, I led Dick Armstrong out on a baptizing tour from Pasadena all across the nation to New York City—zigzagging all along the way to visit people on that route—since Dick had never actually participated on a baptizing tour before. We met George Meeker in New York, and I was able to help Dick and George board the *Queen Mary* and see that great ship, actually going with them into their state room before the ship embarked for Britain. Then I flew down to Washington, D.C. to see that great city that I had never seen before. One of my mother's sisters, "Aunt Glad," lived there and worked for the Civil Service; she helped show me around some and gave me a map with markings of all the key tourist sites of the city. So, I was able to get around and see quite a bit during the two days I was there.

# Chapter 6
## Building a Family and Foundation

Later that summer, I flew to Texas to join Ted Armstrong and take him on a baptizing tour as I had done with Dick. Ted's second son, David, had not yet been born, and we waited a few days until he was born before we left on the tour. As with Dick, Ted had never been an actual participant on a baptizing tour, and because of that—and since I had been his Bible teacher—I was the leader of the tour during the three-and-a-half weeks we spent together in East Texas and Louisiana. Although Ted and I had already liked one another, we became really good friends during that tour, and remained so for years afterward.

On the tour in Louisiana, we walked up one day to a wooden shanty where a lady had written from to ask for baptism. Her husband came out on the front porch and accosted us, yelling, "Where are you boys from?" We said, "We are from Ambassador College in Pasadena." Then he loudly yelled, "Armstrong!" and tried to grab a wooden chair on the front porch to hit us over the head with it. So, we grabbed the chair and did a dance around the front porch with him yelling and screaming at us. Seeing he was getting nowhere, this man began to curse (what a vocabulary he had) and then turned and ran back into the house, yelling, "I'll get the gun!"

Ted and I simply stood on the front steps and prayed for God's protection. We soon realized that the man was bluffing, as he returned with another wooden chair with which to hit us. We were *really* happy to see that chair instead of a gun.

We then got into the front yard and held him—Ted on one arm and I on another—while he cursed and tried to get loose. We soon realized we were going to have to completely knock him out or subdue him if we were going to be able to baptize his wife—and doing so would not be Christian. Soon, his wife came around the edge of the house in her bathing suit and wrapped in a big towel, crying and asking for baptism. I yelled at her several times, "Go up to Big Sandy and see Ken Swisher, and he will baptize you!" She heard me, for we found out later that she did so. Soon, I yelled out to Ted—since it was his day to drive—"Get the car ready!" As the two of us had both seen gangster movies and the like, he knew exactly what I meant. So, he started the car and got it all turned around for me to jump in.

I shoved the fellow in the other direction and ran to the car before he could catch me or throw a rock at it, and we made our "getaway." But he did get off one rock, which hit the chrome piece at the back of the car—but it did not do any significant damage. So, we swiftly drove down the road and prayed that God would help this dear lady be able to be baptized by going up to Big Sandy, where a local minister could do it. Again, we found out later that she was able to do this. As I have related before about this tour and others, we were met by a variety of threats like this—including having guns pointed at us on several occasions. We had to put our faith and trust in God and know that He would take care of us.

**Courting Margie McNair**
After the tour with Ted, I flew up to Joplin, Missouri to spend a few days with my parents. While I was there, I got a call from Mr. Armstrong, asking me to fly up to Chicago and perform the wedding of Raymond McNair and his bride-to-be. Mr. Armstrong had planned to perform the wedding, but business had come up that made it difficult, so he asked me to do it. I gladly acquiesced, as I loved Raymond, and flew to Chicago to stay with Raymond in his apartment until the Sabbath.

It also turned out that Margie McNair, Raymond's younger sister, had come to attend the wedding and was staying with Leona, his bride-to-be. So, on the Thursday night when I arrived, the four of us went to a nice Italian restaurant and had a very long, wonderful visit—made even more special by Margie's presence, for I remembered how

## Building a Family and Foundation

this beautiful young farm girl had come bouncing in from the field to help set the table and visit with us when Raymond and I were there to visit her folks in 1951, and again in 1952 when I came to her home with Burk McNair. My interest increased greatly as I saw her again, looking more beautiful than ever. I was getting "lonesome" and really beginning to want to get married and have a companion.

After I performed Raymond's wedding, it worked out that Margie and I went back to Pasadena together on the train. As we sat together during the overnight trip and had long talks, I began to realize how wonderful it would be to have her as my life's companion. The train stopped in Pasadena before heading on to the main station in Los Angeles, and we were met by Bill Homberger and Annie Mann, the Mayfair House mother. Mrs. Mann told us later that she had "sensed" something was up when she saw me get off the train with Margie.

Indeed, something was up, and I began to date Margie nonstop the rest of that summer and on through the autumn, marrying her in late November of 1955. We ended up having four beautiful children together, and I have always been grateful that God granted her to me as my wife in those early years. I was a very intense person and could have been a little bit difficult for some girls to get along with, yet Margie knew me well, as her older brothers were good friends with me and all of us already seemed like "family" in a certain sense, so she was not overwhelmed by my intensity. We had a wonderful honeymoon and many happy years together as she helped me travel all over the country and over the British Isles, helping "build the Work" as we both wanted to do.

As the time drew near for Margie and me to marry, I asked Ted and Shirley Armstrong to go with me to Bullock's Department store and help pick out the engagement ring and wedding ring—as I had no experience with such things. They very kindly did this. We had already become good friends and Margie and I had already "double dated" with Ted and Shirley a few times before our marriage, also having many meals and social occasions afterward in those early days. Ted sang at my wedding the piece I requested: "I'll Walk with God." It became one of my favorite pieces in those early days and has always been a type of theme for my life.

Right after the wedding, we all walked up to Mayfair just before the "wedding feast," which Mrs. Mann had helped put on for us. Mr.

Armstrong came over to Margie and me and enthusiastically asked my new bride, "Margie, how does it feel to be Mrs. McNair?" Margie was a little stunned and said, "No, Mr. Armstrong, it is now Mrs. *Meredith.*" Mr. Armstrong quickly recovered, apologized, and never made that mistake again. It shows that we are all human—I have done the same type of thing on several occasions.

Interestingly, before my marriage to Margie, the "four bachelors" on the faculty at Ambassador College were Dick Armstrong, Benjamin Rea, Dibar Apartian, and me. Dr. Rea was teaching International Relations and Spanish, and he later became the first Dean of the Ambassador College campus in Bricket Wood, England. Mr. Apartian was *very* new, as he had just arrived that summer of 1955, hired as a French instructor by Dick Armstrong. He knew nothing about the truth until that time. But we all got to know each other very well, sometimes ate out together, and "enjoyed" our bachelorhood to a degree—though, soon after I got married, the others began to do so also. Dr. Rea was my "best man" at the wedding and Mr. Apartian filled in as his assistant, helping me in various ways at that time. We became very good friends, even back then.

Just a few weeks after Margie and I returned from our honeymoon, the professor who taught speech at Ambassador College suddenly eloped with one of the students. This professor was not a member of the Church—and, more importantly, he was already *married.* This being so, Mr. Armstrong had to fire him and disfellowship that student—and that sad event left the Speech Department without a leader.

What to do?

Though I was already teaching three Bible classes, writing for our two magazines, and pastoring the San Diego congregation on weekends, besides other responsibilities, Mr. Armstrong asked *me* of all people to immediately take over the Speech Department. I was a little overwhelmed, but I did the best I could. Looking back on this later, I realized that—with limited budget, the small student body, and other factors—I may have been the best choice under the circumstances. Also, as Mr. Armstrong may have learned previously, I'd had a speech class in Junior High School, another speech class in Senior High, another class in Joplin Junior College, and one more speech class at Ambassador College under Walter Dillon, Mr. Armstrong's brother-in-law, who was an outstanding instructor in speech. So, I certainly had a background in various approaches to teaching the subject.

With two Speech classes added to my responsibilities along with the theology classes, the "honeymoon months" of my marriage were cut very short. However, I had already sincerely given my life to God, and I *meant* it. Margie understood and was very supportive—though I was extremely busy from then on in "the Work," as we called all the activities of the Radio Church of God and Ambassador College.

**Helping Mr. Armstrong Expand the Work**
It was about that time that Mrs. Armstrong recruited me to help her warn her husband about the "phonies" who would often take advantage of him. Since he was very trusting of people, she'd had to do this all alone, and so she came to me one day and said, "Rod, I see that you are very loyal to Mr. Armstrong and very perceptive of people and their attitudes. Maybe the *two* of us could cooperate in warning Mr. Armstrong about these people taking advantage of my husband's trusting spirit." I was glad to do this, and it was wonderful to be able to work with her in this way—and *try* to do so even after her death.

During the early summer of 1956—while the Armstrongs were in Europe—the wonderful property of Hulett C. Merritt became available to us. It was a magnificent mansion on South Orange Grove, and Mr. Armstrong had always felt that he could not afford it. Besides, Mr. Merritt had *not* wanted "that Armstrong" to gain possession of this property. However, Mr. Merritt had just died, and the property was being sold at a public auction—with a realtor, somehow, giving us first opportunity to obtain it if we wished. So, I telephoned Mr. Armstrong immediately about this amazing opportunity to see what he would decide. I was, as I have explained, helping him in many decisions involving the Work of God.

Mr. Armstrong explained the situation in his own autobiography, on pages 395–397 of volume 2:

> While we were in London on this 1956 tour, before leaving for the Middle East, I received a trans-Atlantic telephone call from Mr. Meredith at Pasadena headquarters. It was near midnight in London—but shortly before 5 p.m. in Pasadena. He asked me whether I felt the college would like to

acquire the estate of multimillionaire Hulett C. Merritt.... Mr. Meredith explained that the executor of the estate was going to put it on the market, but first, privately, it was being offered to us through an insurance and real estate broker and his associates.... "Could you gain access to the place yet tonight?," I asked. Mr. Meredith said they could.... The telegram was waiting for me on arising next morning. The ornate and fabulous building would be ideally suited to become our chief classroom building of the college. I telegraphed the decision: Accept it.

Later, in the summer of 1956, Mr. Armstrong directed Dick and me to conduct an evangelistic campaign in Fresno, California, to really get things going up there. The congregation was *very* small, and through our five-week campaign of six nights per week, its size was tripled or quadrupled. It was a wonderful experience to speak on prophetic and related topics night after night, and Mr. Armstrong seemed very pleased with our efforts. Again, Dick and I—now along with Margie— were thrown close together and enjoyed working with one another a great deal. After the Feast of Tabernacles that autumn—now being conducted on the property that had been donated by the Roy Hammer family in Big Sandy, Texas—Margie and I were sent to London, England, to fully establish and solidify the Church of God there.

Mr. Armstrong had conducted a small campaign there that summer. But after his absence, attendance had dropped to an average of only *four* people—besides the young men left behind to run the little office we had there. So, Margie and I went all over London visiting people, encouraging those who had already attended Mr. Armstrong's previous campaigns to "come back" to Sabbath services. In January of 1957, I got permission from Mr. Armstrong to conduct my own smaller campaign in a meeting room of the Royal Empire Society just off Trafalgar Square in London. A variety of people came into the Church through that campaign, including Robin Jones, later a minister in the Church, and James Wells, who also became a minister in the Church and later a faithful elder in the Living Church of God.

As it had been decided that I would return that spring to Pasadena to continue teaching and helping Mr. Armstrong, Mr. Gerald Waterhouse—one of my former students—was sent over to London to

# Building a Family and Foundation

replace me in carrying on the small London congregation, which was now beginning to grow. Soon after he came, my daughter Elizabeth was born in London. I was, for the first time, a father—the father of a beautiful little girl. She added a great deal of joy to my wife and me. Then we returned to Pasadena, where I was to continue teaching, writing, and assisting Mr. Armstrong and Ted in running the Work.

That summer, Herman Hoeh and my Uncle Paul went on a tour to the Middle East, Asia, and later Africa. It was during that time—while he was overseas—that my uncle's wife, my Aunt Ethel, suddenly died after a serious fall. It was a stressful time for me, as I tried again and again to contact Uncle Paul, calling and sending telegrams to his destinations in the Middle East. But as often happens in that part of the world, my messages did not get delivered. He went on traveling without knowing that his wife was dead. Finally, after a week or so of this, we had to bury Aunt Ethel. I performed the funeral, and my uncle was absolutely *shattered* when he and Mr. Hoeh came back through London and found out from Gerald Waterhouse that his wife had been dead and buried now for weeks.

On a happier note, I had the privilege of ordaining Mr. Harold Jackson as a deacon in the Church—of course, with Mr. Armstrong's permission. Mr. Jackson and I became very dear friends over the years, and he was Margie's last "dinner guest" in our home in La Cañada.

During the winter of 1957–58, I continued helping Mr. Armstrong and Ted direct the Work. It was somewhere during this period that Mr. Raymond Cole was made Director of the Ministry. He seemed to work at this fairly well at first, but later discord arose between him and Ted Armstrong because he did not communicate well with Ted, as he should have done. At this point, Raymond got Mr. Armstrong's permission to move Church Administration all the way up to Eugene, Oregon—which meant that Church Administration was *separated* from Headquarters. Of course, this brought about serious problems later.

Meanwhile, I had been working on my master's degree thesis for several years. I had decided to title it *The Plain Truth About the Protestant Reformation*. I was able to finish it during this time, and so received my master's degree in Theology—after taking all the required class hours and finishing the thesis in the spring of 1958. That summer, Mr. Armstrong sent Raymond McNair and his wife, Leona, to Britain to replace Mr. Waterhouse in directing the Work in England.

Gerald Waterhouse was sent to South Africa to get the Work going down there. So, Mr. and Mrs. Raymond McNair spent the next fifteen solid *years* in Great Britain building the Work. Mr. Raymond McNair was my wife's own brother and he and I were very close for many years. Many of our older brethren will remember the quiet service, dedication, and sound biblical teachings Mr. McNair gave them. Mr. McNair built *strongly* upon the foundation for the Work that we had already laid in the United Kingdom. Incidentally, he was the one who discovered the property where we later established the Ambassador College branch in Britain, Hanstead House near Bricket Wood. It was the home of a multi-millionaire who had helped build the East India Company for many years before eventually retiring to this beautiful estate in the "Greenbelt" about 19 miles north of London.

# Chapter 7

## Trials and Encouragement

During the summer of 1958, Dick Armstrong—having been made acting pastor of the Headquarters congregation in Pasadena, California—was granted several unusual miracles by Almighty God. The most outstanding miracle occurred over Pentecost weekend in 1958. I had been to Chicago to conduct Pentecost services for brethren in that growing area. Upon my return, I was met by one of the young college men who was in our Transportation Department. Upon meeting me, he asked, "Mr. Meredith, have you heard about Howard Clark's healing?"

I was astonished, for Howard Clark had been a quadriplegic for several years, having been severely injured by shrapnel during the Korean War. As a Marine, he had been sent to many top Navy hospitals and given the very best treatment they could give him—all to no avail. He was considered doomed to spend the rest of his life as a quadriplegic, hardly able to move or get around. I remember that he sat for *years* on the left side of the audience looking toward the stage in the hall we rented for the Headquarters Sabbath services for many years. As I was preaching, I could always see Howard sitting there in his wheelchair, and he had to be helped in and out of a special station wagon equipped to hold that wheelchair. He was always very friendly and positive, despite being very seriously handicapped and unable to do much at all for many years. I would talk to him to encourage him often. In fact, I had baptized him and gotten to know him quite well.

Now he was supernaturally *healed*. For him to be immediately healed was indeed an outstanding miracle—one that I will never, ever forget. The next day after my return from Chicago, as I came over to the campus before classes, there was Howard Clark sitting on the fender of his car. I was surprised at even this, though I had heard he had been healed—for Howard had been unable to even balance himself enough to sit in a chair without arms or braces of some sort. He smiled at me as I came toward him in the parking lot. He had a twinkle in his eye, as he knew *exactly* what I was thinking. I said, "Howard, I hear you have been absolutely healed through Dick Armstrong's prayers."

He said, "Yes, I have." And he kept just sitting there on the fender of the car. I kind of looked sideways and Howard, again, understood what I was thinking. "You want to see me walk, don't you?"

"Of course!" I said. Smiling, he got down from the fender and lumbered slowly around the car all on his own—no cane or crutches—though he went slowly and unsteadily at first, as his muscles took several weeks to adjust to his healing. But Howard *was* healed. And I tell all of you reading this before Almighty God that I know it was a supernatural miracle, for I deeply inquired into the circumstances, as I often do with this type of thing. I am from Missouri—the "Show Me State"—so, when people tell me they have been "healed," I sometimes ask about the details. If they have had a bad cold and simply drank orange juice and water for several days before it finally went away, I do not regard that as supernatural healing—or anything *else* of that nature. But if it has been medically diagnosed by physicians and medical tests, and *then* Almighty God heals—then I know.

Almighty God again showed—through the prayers of Richard David Armstrong—that He could heal and *did* heal powerfully and dramatically. It was very, very inspiring to *hundreds of us* who knew Howard and had been very aware of his situation for several years.

However, near the end of July, Dick Armstrong and Don Billingsley were going on a baptizing tour and got into a head-on crash at mid-morning near San Luis Obispo, California. Mr. Billingsley thought that the highway was two lanes in each direction. Yet, as they came up over a little rise and were passing another car on their right, suddenly a big Cadillac was heading *right* for them. Mr. Billingsley could not swerve to the right because of the car he was passing, so he swerved to the left to hit the ditch. But he was not able to do this in time to avoid this oncoming larger car from smashing directly into the "death seat" where Dick was sitting. Dick's body was *crushed*, and he never recovered—though he spent several days in the local hospital.

Checking on it later, Norman Smith—who was *very* intelligent and very methodical—drove back and forth in the area and found that it was obvious that the Highway Department had not properly marked the signs. Because the signs were mislabeled as they were, we *could* have sued the state of California for this mistake. Mr. Smith went back to the accident site and proved that this was the case.

At any rate, as it turned out, soon after this crash occurred, I was sitting directly across from Mr. Armstrong's desk in his small "penthouse office" on the third floor of the library building. I can't remember what we were talking about. But I will never, ever forget the following conversation and the look on Mr. Armstrong's face. He answered the phone, and it was Don Billingsley, crying as he called. He told Mr. Armstrong about the crash and that he himself had been injured but felt the need to call very quickly. He then described in detail how seriously Dick was injured and how he was lying at death's door in the local hospital there. Seeing Mr. Armstrong's reaction as Don was telling him about what had just happened to his son was enlightening to me. I could see the wheels of Mr. Armstrong's brain whirling, so to speak. He then turned and said to me, "Rod, Dick is near death in the hospital up there and Mrs. Armstrong and I need to go immediately." Right while I was sitting there, he tried to call and rent or lease a private plane to fly up right away. He could not do so without a lot of financial checking out and raising money, etc. So, he then decided to have Norman Smith—director of our radio studio—drive him up and be there with him during all the time necessary.

## Dick Armstrong's Death

Mr. Armstrong, as a man of God, even tried to encourage Don to be faithful and carry on. Then, after he hung up and thought for a few minutes, he told me, "Rod, with Ted back in the Springfield, Missouri, campaign, there is no one here to lead the Work properly except you, as Mrs. Armstrong and I are going up there right away to be with Dick. I will have Norman Smith drive us up, as I am afraid that in my emotional condition, I should not drive that entire long trip anyway. So, you carry on here—direct the Work in all normal ways and call me if there is any emergency. But I know you will take care of things over the next several days as God guides you. I may be a week or two or more up there." So, I was given that responsibility at that time—a little preview of what I would later have when I was made Second Vice President of the Worldwide Church of God and Ambassador College after Dick's death.

After about a week in the local hospital, Dick died as he was being transferred by ambulance down from San Luis Obispo to the UCLA Medical Center. His body was then brought over to the Turner Stevens Mortuary in Pasadena. Since Mr. Armstrong knew that Dick and I had been dear friends, he asked me to accompany him to the mortuary soon after Dick's body arrived. As we went in and found Dick's body on the "slab"—I think it is called—still not prepared for burial, I suggested strongly to Mr. Armstrong that we lay hands on Dick and pray *fervently*, even then, that God would raise him from the dead.

I was still new in the truth, in a sense, and had a great deal of youthful enthusiasm and childlike faith. Mr. Armstrong agreed, and we fervently prayed that God would raise Dick right then. However, it was not to be. Even during the funeral—conducted by Mr. Armstrong himself—I looked up to Mount Wilson just above Mountain View Cemetery and prayed that God would raise up Dick right then. But it was not God's will to do so at that time. It was best in His perfect will to let Dick sleep until the resurrection.

Also, since Dick and his wife, Lois, had both been close to Margie and me, in her sorrow Lois came over to stay with Margie at our home a few days later when I took Dr. Benjamin Rea on a baptizing tour. It gave Lois a little comfort and companionship during that time to be with Margie, who was always a very friendly, compassionate, and positive person. The baptizing tour took about three weeks of traveling through Northern California and Southern Oregon. Dr. Rea had not had that opportunity before. He and I were good friends, but he had never been on a baptizing tour. So, we had a fruitful tour—though sorrowfully colored somewhat, being so soon after Dick's death.

But even in times of stress and sorrow, God often gives us some encouragement. And I, personally, had a *great* deal of encouragement during those days of August 1958, with the birth of my first *son,* Michael Rea Meredith. Mike was born August 13, 1958, in our little home on a hill overlooking the fire station in La Cañada, California.

It gave me a great deal of encouragement to have a son born during this time to offset the other trials that were occurring. And Mike has always been a very interesting and intelligent person—and very loyal and helpful to me, personally. He later earned the respect of hundreds of his coworkers through his capacity to work with people and get things done. I am thankful to have had *four* sons. But Mike was my first son, so I will never forget the time of his birth and what it meant at that point.

**Made Second Vice President**

That autumn, with Dick's death and with Ted alone left to carry on in case Mr. Armstrong himself died, Mr. Herbert Armstrong appointed me as Second Vice President of the Radio Church of God and Ambassador College. I recall that, soon after I was appointed, Mr. Armstrong instructed me to go around the entire campus, look in on all the departments, and understand at least their basic functions, "just in case" I had to take over if something happened to him and to Ted—who was already Executive Vice President. Those of you who have collected old Church publications over the years may be interested to know that there was even an article about this in the congregational newspaper published by the zealous and loyal brethren in Chicago, Illinois.

From then on, I was included even more in virtually all the top-level meetings involving the Work and Ambassador College. This included buying radio time, making decisions about major property acquisitions, and many other matters, certainly including spiritual decisions that I had already been involved in for years as one of the pioneer students and instructors at the college. It was a wonderful opportunity to be so intimately associated with Mr. Armstrong in managing the entire Work and college for the next fifteen years. During those years, a great deal of growth occurred. Also, capable older students—some even veterans from World War II—came to Ambassador. Many of them were older and more impressive and capable than me, and God did use many of them in important positions in the Work. This included such men as Albert J. Portune, Charles F. Hunting, Leslie McCullough, and others. Yet I had the opportunity to teach them theology classes, get to know them better, often counsel and encourage them, and in many cases *recommend* them for the vital positions they later held in the Work. Later, I laughingly told some of the other ministers and teachers to "be nice" to the newer men they were training, for "they may become your *bosses* later on."

Interestingly, despite his claims, a man named Stanley Rader was virtually unknown during those early years of the Work. From the mid-1950s onward, he began to come over from Los Angeles to our offices to help in the accounting area for a few hours a week. Later, he would come for two or three days a week. But he was certainly not "running" anything or acting as Mr. Armstrong's advisor in anything besides that limited function. Only after Mrs. Armstrong's death in 1967 did Mr. Rader begin to be consistently employed at our Pasadena offices. It was during those years—in the late 1960s and 1970s—that he began to have a great deal of influence on Mr. Armstrong, especially after Mrs. Armstrong's death. He and Ted Armstrong were often at loggerheads as to who would have the greater influence in various situations. Many of us at Headquarters fervently wished that Mrs. Armstrong were still alive, as she would have given very good counsel to her husband.

Early in January 1959, a beautiful banquet was conducted in the sumptuous Rosewood Room of Ambassador Hall. It was to celebrate the 25th anniversary of the *World Tomorrow* radio broadcast. Of course, Mr. and Mrs. Herbert W. Armstrong were the honored guests. After the very fine meal, Ted Armstrong and others proposed "toasts" honoring Mr. Armstrong for establishing this Work and for all his accomplishments. Even the Vice Mayor of Pasadena was there and offered kind words. Then, our advertising representative got up and gave many flowery praises to Mr. Armstrong and all that he had done. Sitting near Mr. Armstrong and seeing him beginning to crouch down and clear his throat, I instinctively knew that an explosion was coming.

Soon after the last series of laudatory comments, Mr. Armstrong stood up and graciously thanked the other guests for coming and for their kind words. But then, suddenly, he exploded. He startled the invited guests by loudly stating with great conviction, "My friends, you all need to realize that Herbert Armstrong did not build this Work! It was the living Jesus Christ who built this Work through a weak, puny servant, Herbert W. Armstrong. God had to knock me down again and again and humble me before God could even use me—as weak as I am. So, I want all of you to understand that this truly is the Work of God and not of *any man!*"

Everyone sat in stunned silence. The outside dignitaries had obviously never heard anything like this before. But even the unconverted guests sensed the *total* sincerity of Mr. Armstrong's powerful comments. This gave all of us something to think about for the rest of our lives.

So, although Mr. Armstrong often appeared to be supremely confident and often did show a lot of human nature, I came to realize that, deep down, he was *totally* committed to giving his life to God and preaching the full truth of the Bible no matter *what.* There were many times through the years when I saw him, in total sincerity, acknowledge that he himself was weak and that he could do nothing apart from God's help. It is something for all of us to think about. Mr. Armstrong was totally committed in every fiber of his being to do one thing with complete confidence: preach the complete *biblical* truth, not "watering down" anything or turning aside from what the Bible actually *said.* I saw that full sincerity and commitment in his sermons, Bible classes, and personal conversations.

Mr. Armstrong *would* make human mistakes from time to time. But he occasionally said to some of us in private, "Though I may make many personal mistakes, I have committed myself to preach the real truth of the Bible no matter what." Through the decades, I found that to be an *absolutely* true statement. I also came to realize over the decades—from meetings and from hearing and reading about many so-called "Christian" leaders—that they are usually very political and very concerned about what people think. As the Bible tells us, it was the same way in Jesus' time, for the Apostle John said of the rulers of the Pharisees who would not confess their belief in Christ, "They loved the praise of men more than the praise of God" (John 12:43).

As 1959 progressed, my own teaching and writing responsibilities continued until mid-summer. At that time, Mr. Armstrong sent me and my wife to San Antonio, Texas, to conduct an evangelistic campaign there for our *World Tomorrow* listeners and others. The local congregation was losing members rapidly and a "revival" was needed. Our local minister, though sincere and clean cut, was simply not a "people person" and had a great deal of emotional baggage—he did not really belong in the ministry. Later, we transferred him to another responsibility.

During this evangelistic campaign, I was assisted by Mr. Al Portune as song leader along with my own sister—now Mrs. Kathryn Ames—who played violin while another student named Ruth Myrick played the piano. This campaign was an old-style campaign that Mr. Armstrong had outlined for us; it was conducted six nights a week for four solid weeks. Therefore, I preached 24 sermons in a row, plus preaching on the Sabbath and sometimes *twice* on the Sabbath, as we would sometimes go down to Corpus Christi, Texas, in the morning and return to San Antonio for the afternoon services. Quite a few people came into the Church of God through the campaign, and the local congregation regained most of the members it had lost, along with some others as well.

Dr. & Mrs. Benjamin (Hazel) Rea

After these meetings and after visiting my parents in Joplin, I was back at work teaching at the college and helping Mr. Armstrong administer the Work. It was during this year that I assisted him in deciding that Dr. Benjamin Rea would be the first dean of Ambassador College and giving input about other leaders for the Work there in Britain. During this time, he discussed the "spirit in man"—as it was soon after Dick's death and his mind was very heavily on what happened to a person after death. During those years, Mr. Armstrong would often rehearse over and *over* any basic doctrine he was studying into. He would preach on it and talk about it in other meetings, and other situations. And it was obvious that he was very *deep* in his thinking about such things and turned them over and over in his mind, praying about them until he became very sure of what was the full truth on a variety of basic matters that the world's "Christianity" does not truly understand.

# Chapter 8
## Expanding Horizons

In the spring of 1960, I was once again sent to the United Kingdom, this time to conduct *three* evangelistic campaigns in a row. It turned out that I gave about 67 sermons over a twelve-week period—including preaching twice at times in the local congregations on weekends. The *purpose* of these campaigns was to raise up local congregations in Bristol, Birmingham, and Manchester, England. Small Bible Study groups had already been established by Raymond McNair, but Mr. Armstrong wanted me to reach out more publicly, bring more people from our mailing list, and develop proper congregations. We were able to do so, and those local groups existed for many years until the Worldwide Church began to come apart. That autumn, I remained in England to help Mr. Armstrong establish the British branch of Ambassador College at Bricket Wood. I taught the Freshman Bible classes and Epistles of Paul classes and was made "Athletic Director" for the first semester I was there.

My second son, James Paul Meredith, was born right on the campus in what we called the "Rose Cottages," where some of the faculty lived. These were old, tiny—by American standards—stone duplexes with old fireplaces where you had to burn charcoal, and they had *no* air conditioning and *no* central heating. However, most of us during those years were very *accustomed* to sacrificing and no one complained, for our lives were given to God, and if we'd had to live in tents to do the "Work" we would certainly have done that.

With Jim's birth there at Bricket Wood, it turned out that two of my six children were born right in Britain. I have *always* had a special feeling for the British people since I helped Dick and Mr. Armstrong start the Work there in 1954, helped establish and strengthen the London congregation in 1956–57, and then was used by Christ to establish the congregations in Bristol, Birmingham, and Manchester—plus the British branch of Ambassador College at Bricket Wood in 1960.

During that autumn, Mr. Armstrong asked me whether I would like to stay there in Britain as Director of the Work there and as Deputy Chancellor of the college, or return to Pasadena to teach, write, and help him administer the Work. It was a lesson of being willing to put my life totally in God's hands and go wherever I was sent.

With Raymond McNair during a baptizing tour, December 1960

It truly was hard to be sure, because as Mr. Armstrong explained, "Over in Britain you would be a big duck in a small pond." Yet in Pasadena, I would simply be a member of the top team in the general Work. But I told Mr. Armstrong that I sincerely wanted him to make the decision and he later decided to bring me back to Pasadena.

However, before I returned, Mr. Armstrong sent Raymond McNair and me on a baptizing tour to South Africa. We were the first Radio Church of God ministers to visit Africa, a continent largely untouched by the true Gospel, and it was a special opportunity to meet the wonderful people there in South Africa—as well as in what was then called Northern Rhodesia—to baptize those who had requested it. As it turned out, we baptized *three* brethren in Northern Rhodesia and 21 in the Union of South Africa. We had not even returned to Bricket Wood before we heard that Gerald Waterhouse was proclaiming that a *double* foundation had been laid, because Mr. Armstrong had always taught that the number twelve was the number of organizational beginnings and we had just baptized 24 people—two times twelve—on our tour.

Returning through Rome, we decided to see that great city, as Raymond had never visited Rome before. Through the American Embassy, we were able to obtain tickets to sit in the press gallery during the Christmas extravaganza where Pope John XXIII would be right in the middle of things in Saint Peter's Basilica. It was truly an educational experience—somewhat like the experience that Dick and I had at Castel Gandolfo. Rather than speaking from a high balcony, Pope John XXIII was carried about on a portable throne by about eight men who moved it around so he could see the crowd from different directions with people yelling, screaming, and shouting "Viva Papa, Viva Papa," over and over. Again, an attitude of absolute worship was very evident in those confused individuals.

### Appointed Director of the Ministry

In early January, Margie and I—now with three children—flew home with Mr. and Mrs. Herbert Armstrong, refueling in Gander, Newfoundland, on the way to Los Angeles. Mrs. Armstrong had graciously agreed to switch seats and to sit with Margie so that I could spend a lot of time with Mr. Armstrong and discuss the possibility of a *second* Feast site in the United States. He had always felt that everyone had to come to one place because of the intimation of certain scriptures in the Old Testament. But, having taught the Epistles of Paul class and having wondered for years where the *Gentile* Christians at Corinth and Ephesus and other places would have gone for the Feast—as *all* Christians are to keep the Feasts of God (Zechariah 14:16–19)—I discussed this matter with Dr. Hoeh. He and I came to realize that there *had* to be a place besides Jerusalem for Gentile Christians to attend. After I explained this in great detail to Mr. Armstrong on our long trip home—along with other matters—he wholeheartedly agreed that this made sense.

He gave me permission to have our men look for a second Feast site located near the West Coast so that our brethren there would not have to travel across the deserts and plains to the site in Big Sandy, East Texas. So, after talking with Ted Armstrong after I got back, we sent Les McCullough and Ron Kelly up to central California to look for a Feast site in a more central area for our brethren out there. I suggested the possibility of the California State Fairgrounds in Sacramento. However, nothing worked out there, so Messrs. McCullough and Kelly eventually came up with the possibility of having the Feast at Squaw Valley, California.

This turned out to be a fine site, as it had been the venue for the Winter Olympics held the previous year. *Thousands* of our brethren will always remember the interesting and beautiful Feast site at Squaw Valley.

Later, we established a *third* Feast site on Jekyll Island, Georgia. These three sites—Jekyll Island on the East Coast, Big Sandy in the midsection of the country, and Squaw Valley near the West Coast—all were perfectly situated apart from each other to give easier access for the brethren across the United States to attend the Feast regularly.

Coming back to Pasadena, Margie and I were placed in a small rental home for a couple of years or so, for even though I was Second Vice President of the growing Work, all of us were on fairly small salaries and had to live modestly in order to stretch the budget of the Work and keep the Work and the college growing in every possible way. We were sincerely happy to do this, as *none* of us, to my knowledge, came to Ambassador College or into the ministry to get ahead financially. In fact, there *were* no finances, so to speak, in the early years of the college. Things were very tight, and we often had to go to Vern Mattson, the Business Manager, and beg to get a check so we could pay our rent just before the landlady kicked us out or to have money to buy an engagement ring or wedding ring, as I did when I married Margie. In those years, we had to learn to truly live by faith.

At this time, however, with the Work growing swiftly and the number of congregations and ministers increasing, it became increasingly evident that it was not efficient for the Church Administration Department to be conducted from up in Eugene, Oregon. Also, by that time, though Ted Armstrong had urgently requested that Raymond Cole check in with him and others at Headquarters on various things, this was not happening. So, Ted ended up getting his father to appoint *me* as Superintendent of Ministers for the United States and Canada. Ted himself, at first, directed the international offices and local congregations. Later, he took over the Canadian Work as well, and appointed Mr. Dean Wilson as the first Director of the Work in Canada.

After being appointed Superintendent of Ministers for the United States and Canada, I was *extremely* busy, to say the least, for I still had all my classes to teach, articles to write, obligations to fulfill in various meetings and situations as Second Vice President of the Work, etc. At *no* time did I ever seek to be Superintendent of Ministers. I had helped teach most of these men and knew them rather well, but I was, frankly,

## Expanding Horizons

Dr. Meredith ca. 1969

too busy doing all these *other* things to have time and energy to devote myself fully as a manager in running the Church Administration Department.

In the first half of 1961, I helped raise up our local church in Bakersfield, California. Little did I realize that, years later, a beautiful young widow from that very congregation would become my wife—though I never met Sheryl until after Margie's death in 1976. Also, in the summer of 1961, I took Mr. Dibar Apartian on a baptizing tour through northern California and southern Oregon, as I had done with Dr. Benjamin Rea.

All through those years, Mr. Apartian and I were becoming very close friends, and we remained that way until his death in 2010. God was beginning to use him to raise up the "French Work"—as we called it—serving the brethren in France, Eastern Canada, and French-speaking parts of the Caribbean. During those years, Ted Armstrong and I continued as pretty good friends, and I accompanied him on camping trips in the High Sierras, water skiing out on the Salton Sea, and other enjoyable activities. Also, Herman Hoeh and I continued to work together for hundreds of hours getting out *The Plain Truth* and *The Good News* magazines as well as booklets, and we became even deeper friends and associates over the decades.

During those years, I recommended Dr. Rea as the first Dean of Ambassador College in Britain. He did a fine job there until his untimely death early in 1965. I also recommended Charles Hunting as the Business Manager for the Work in Britain, and Mr. Al Portune as the Business Manager for the entire Work in Pasadena after Vern Mattson's departure. I had the privilege of regularly giving counsel to Mr. Armstrong about situations involving leading men, their problems, and where they would fit in the Work of God.

About this time, an outstanding young man named Richard Ames, already graduated from Rensselaer Polytechnic Institute, came to Ambassador College in the autumn of 1962. He was a leader among the students and a very dedicated individual, and he graduated in the spring of 1965 as Student Body President during his senior year. He married my sister Kathryn, then went immediately into the field ministry and successfully served there for some time before being transferred to Big Sandy as a faculty member, and later to Pasadena in the same capacity.

## Our Educators Tour

David Jon Hill—an outstanding teacher, preacher, and writer with an unusually scintillating personality—accompanied me on an around-the-world trip during the summer of 1963. We decided to take this trip because we found that this "Educators Tour" was sponsored and *subsidized* by the Scandinavian Airlines and the American Book Company for college teachers. Obviously, they hoped, by giving us a greatly reduced rate, to introduce us to their own businesses so we would buy their books and travel with them more in the future. Nevertheless, it was a wonderful opportunity and it turned out to be even more exciting than we had imagined when we had first planned this trip.

Originally, there were supposed to be a few *dozen* educators traveling together. However, as tension began to build in the Middle East and a Ba'ath revolt in Syria was threatened, the number of teachers planning the trip fell away and we ended up having only *four* others accompany us on this trip. It did lend itself, however, to a more intimate relationship with the other professors and we learned a great deal from them by being with them literally *all* day long—usually traveling in the same old Chrysler or Cadillac limousine rented by the travel service, staying in the same hotel, eating together, etc. Although I had realized many of these things in theory, I came to *deeply* understand how "out of touch" many of the liberal, bookish, college intellectuals become. At times they seemed to be cut off from actual reality.

One of the older members of our tour was a lady named Dorothy, who taught at Harvard. She was very nice and overall polite, but thought that men and women were "totally the same." As we had become friends and "associates"—literally talking with each other all day long—I kidded her about this from time to time. I said, "Well, Dorothy, if we are *totally* the same, why don't you get the toughest woman on the earth, and I will put her in the ring with Muhammad Ali and see who wins the boxing match?"

Of course, our Arab guides along the way were very amused with this, as they had a very low opinion of women no matter what area of life we might be talking about. But Dorothy seemed to be learning something even from *me*, and she became willing to acknowledge that men have more "upper body strength" and certain other things that make us "different"—although, with her, it didn't go much beyond that.

We got to see Athens and the area around it, as well as the ancient city of Corinth, walking up and down some of the very areas where the Apostle Paul may have walked nearly 2,000 years earlier. It was very inspiring and stirring to see these places mentioned in the Bible. As we came into Damascus, I gradually noticed an increasing number of cars that seemed to be speeding away from the city. Then we began to hear machine gun fire. It seemed that the intellectual professors were not keeping up with world news, as I always did *wherever* I was. I realized immediately that the Ba'ath revolt must already be underway and that our lives would be in danger if we got into the center of the city, where fighting would perhaps be fierce.

I strongly instructed the Arab driver to turn around and get out of the city, telling him what was probably about to happen. He understood and *vigorously* agreed, for *his* life was also obviously in danger. The others in the party grumbled about this at first, but as we came up toward the top of a little hill we had descended only a few minutes earlier, we were confronted right in the middle of the highway by a big tank, whose guns were pointed *right* at our car. We had to stop. Our Arab guide got out and—speaking in Arabic—vigorously enjoined the tank commander and his crew about how we were tourists and Americans, so they grudgingly waved us by, and we were able to make our escape before the rebellion got completely underway. We read about it in the paper at our next stop and were able to ask others in the hotel what had happened. What I feared might happen had indeed taken place. Our lives would have been in danger if I had not been keeping up with world news.

Soon, we were able to visit Jordan and got to see the ancient "Rose-Red City" of Petra. It was quite a sight and an experience I will never forget. Many of us have thought of the *possibility* of Petra being the "place of safety" for God's people during the coming great tribulation. Mr. Herbert Armstrong always said that if the Bible indicated a specific place, that place was Petra. However, he said, the Bible was *not* specific and so we must not base our hopes on this one place unless or until God makes it plain. So, that is the way we in this Work have left it.

Jon Hill and I stayed in the *only* hotel and guest house within the city of Petra at that time. It was called the Philadelphia Hotel, although it was only a rustic lodge. Since there was no air conditioning—and it was *blazing* hot—Jon Hill simply picked up his mattress from our hotel room, took it outside, and slept on top of a rock all night under the moon. I was concerned about snakes and decided to stay inside to have more peace of mind. But it turned out that Jon was just as safe and was okay the next morning. We were fascinated to be staying in the Philadelphia Hotel, since we were obviously in the Philadelphia era of the Church of God. So, although that *may* have been a coincidence, it was still kind of encouraging and made our trip seem even more special. We had many interesting experiences in the Arab countries throughout the Middle East and were even able to see the pyramids of Egypt. There, Jon Hill and I were photographed sitting on camels and had many other memorable experiences.

Near the end of the "around-the-world" trip—we had paid about $300 extra to continue around the world, as we were already a *third* of the way around the world from Los Angeles—we were able to visit the Church offices in Australia, where I preached in Sydney. Then, we flew to Manila to see our Manila office and get to see Mr. Pedro Ortiguero and his sons, Benjamin and Jeremiah, who were helping in the Work at that time. Then we went home to California through Hawaii, where we were to preach and where we also baptized several people who had been waiting many months for baptism. Coming to Hawaii was very special, as our wives were able to meet us there and we spent the last few days together on those beautiful islands. Finally, we came back to Pasadena and continued our regular responsibilities.

## Expanding Horizons

With mother Mildred, sisters Kathryn and Patricia, and three oldest children James, Michael, and Elizabeth ca. 1962

In Egypt (on second camel from left), summer of 1963

Fishing at Big Sandy in 1970

# Chapter 9

## The Work Moves Forward

In early 1965, Mr. Armstrong sent me back to Bricket Wood, England with my family so I could be the "guest lecturer at Ambassador College" he had promised. He had hoped Ted Armstrong would go there and do that, Ted having become better-acquainted with England and learning to love the nation as Mr. Armstrong did. But Ted never *did* really enjoy England and was unwilling to go. So, of course, I was glad to heed Mr. Armstrong's wishes and took my whole family over there, gone from my home and my classes for about five months. The subtle and not-so-subtle differences between Mr. Armstrong and his son Ted became more and more apparent as each year went by. The above incident was just one of *many* early situations where Ted and his father seemed to go different ways.

Jesus Himself warned that "a man's enemies will be those of his own household" (Matthew 10:36). So, I was blessed by God in being able to perceive that—although very human at times and lacking in respect even from some of his own *family*—Herbert W. Armstrong was *the* most dedicated servant of God on earth during those years and was willing to preach the *full* truth of the Bible no matter what. This helped me to follow his instructions and help build the Work despite trials, setbacks, and sometimes even false accusations.

Returning to Britain during the Spring of 1965 was a good experience and helped me *understand* the workings of the Bricket Wood campus and the Work in Europe better. I found that Charles Hunting, whom I had recommended as Director of Finance for that area, and

Ronald Dart, an outstanding teacher, were both doing a reasonably good job. But I found them to be very pushy and at times seemingly insubordinate to Raymond McNair, who was the actual Director of the Work in Europe. It is interesting that I spotted both of their wrong attitudes back then, for—as with others—this turned out to be a warning signal of what happened later as these men all *rebelled* against Mr. Armstrong. But I did my best to straighten things out in that situation while I was there.

Also, I was busy teaching classes and counseling students—especially the older students who might soon go into the Work. One outstanding young man I counseled quite a bit was named Francis Bergin. Although in my Freshman Bible Class, he was already on the board of several corporations and was a *very* competent young businessman whose father was a millionaire. Francis had a lot of ability and experience, so I tried to encourage him to see the "big picture" about the Work of God, what we were doing, and how important it was. It seemed to help him, as we personally "hit it off." Also, he ended up visiting America several times over the following years—he and I would alternate in taking each other to dinner and enjoying very interesting and profitable visits that enriched both of our lives.

At the end of the spring semester, I was able to take my wife, Margie, at *long* last, on a trip to Europe. Margie had been such a faithful helper and wife all those years and had been to Britain with me by this time on three different occasions—yet had *never* been to the continent before this trip. She had been pregnant and needed to take care of herself in that way during her previous visits to the British Isles. She had seen London and much of Britain with me, but never greater Europe. Also, it had been several years since I had been to the continent to see significant things relating to Bible prophecy and current events, so, it was profitable to get back over there again, for I was writing articles continually in our magazines about prophetic events relating to Europe and preaching about these things in local congregations and Festival sites.

Therefore, at my *own* expense, I took Margie on a three-and-a-half-week trip to the continent, where we were able to visit Paris, Vienna, Zagreb, and Yugoslavia—and then on down to Venice, Italy, on the train. In fact, the entire trip was taken with a set of Euro Rail passes, which allowed us to go all over Europe for 30 days for an affordable price—especially as the American dollar was still quite strong at that time. So, we saw some very interesting sites. It was especially interesting to stay in Zagreb, as that was the only part of the Iron Curtain area I visited, and it was helpful to see life under Soviet rule.

Then we went down through the mountains of Yugoslavia and on down to the coast to Venice, Italy. Venice is very pretty with lots of wonderful and educational things to see. However, I was somewhat astonished at the amount of tipping that seemed to be necessary to get around there. It may interest those who read this to realize that, as we got off the train, we had to tip the fellow who helped us off. Then, another fellow would carry our bags to the dock of the canal, and we would tip him. Then, another fellow would help transfer our bags into the gondola, as we had to get over to Venice by boat. Then, we had to tip the gondolier at the end of the trip, then give another tip to the man helping us up on the docks, then another tip to a fellow carrying our bags on, then another tip to the bellhop who took us up to the room. Then, as we arrived in the room, there was an important-looking fellow rushing around opening windows, dusting things, showing us how to run the TV, etc. He, of course, obviously looked at us expectantly, letting us know in that way that he *also* needed a tip.

*Wow.* I have never gone through such a tipping experience in my entire life before or since.

Anyway, we were able to see Venice and then go on to Rome and see the magnificence of Saint Peter's Basilica and other various historic sites there. I have always been very grateful for that—though Margie died quite young, I had been able to take her on a thorough trip to see Europe, which was very enjoyable for both of us.

## Special Events and Special People

I have mentioned Mr. Richard Ames coming to college as an engineering graduate of Rensselaer Polytechnic Institute. He became the Student Body President and a leader in the college in many ways, graduating in June 1965. In the summer of 1964, he went on a baptizing tour with Frank McCrady over much of the United States, which gave him valuable ministerial experience. Then, on August 12, 1964, he and my sister Kathryn were married after courting for at least two years. They were both a little bit older than the average students, college graduates, and very capable. They have seemed to make an ideal couple for all these many years, and I am very grateful to have Mr. Richard Ames as my brother-in-law and very capable associate. I sometimes kid him about having "run off" with my sister, but it was *I* who performed the ceremony. Mr. Ames continued in college until he graduated in June of 1965, while Kathryn continued teaching music at Imperial Schools until her husband graduated. After graduation, Mr. Ames took Kathryn on a short baptizing tour through parts of Nevada and elsewhere on their way to Akron, Ohio, where he served in the ministry for a short time. Then, they were transferred to Cincinnati, Ohio, where he pastored one of our largest congregations for eleven months before being brought in to teach at Ambassador College in Big Sandy, Texas. Even in Pasadena, Mr. Ames had assisted Mr. Portune in teaching classes, so we brought him to Big Sandy, where there was a need. He ended up spending 1966–77 teaching at the Big Sandy campus. During that time, he also helped establish and *pastor* Texas congregations in Texarkana and Longview.

Meanwhile, I was working to prepare for my doctorate in theology, which I received in June 1966 after *several* years of taking graduate classes—either part-time or full-time—plus writing a thesis. As Ted Armstrong received a doctorate at the same time, he and I both determined *not* to use our "doctor" titles—as it would seem like we were more important than either his father or my Uncle Paul. So, I was always "Mr." to the brethren until Mr. Armstrong *asked* me to use the doctorate title when I was later sent to the Ambassador College campus at Bricket Wood as Deputy Chancellor.

From 1966 to 1969, I continued to oversee the Church Administration Department—writing, teaching, and helping Mr. Armstrong in many, many overall responsibilities. Also, I was made pastor of the Los Angeles congregation, which for a while became the largest single congregation in the world as it ended up being the overflow group for Headquarters until we started meeting on the Ambassador College campus.

## Mr. Joseph Tkach

Because of the strange events that occurred later, it may be helpful at this point to explain how a man named Joseph Tkach came into such prominence. He had been a local deacon in the Chicago congregation for a few years. His wife was very dedicated and solid. Mr. Tkach was a hard worker, but he seemed to lack academic ability and the ability to preach.

However, the District Superintendent—as they were then called—Dean Blackwell recommended strongly that I bring Joe Tkach on the special one-year training program I had introduced for outstanding local elders, feeling this might prepare these men for greater service full-time in the ministry. It was obvious to *many* of us that Mr. Tkach, though a hard worker, did not really fit into the full-time ministry. He greatly lacked academic skills, was unable to give consistently coherent messages, and sometimes failed to explain various passages of the Bible.

Therefore, because we had already brought him in, we kept him around Los Angeles for a few years and simply assigned him to visits and situations where he would not be a problem. We asked him to visit especially older widows and help them in various ways. This enabled him to use his aggressiveness in helping them get special financial help from the various government agencies, etc. But he certainly did not fit into the ministry, preaching, or writing. Mr. Al Carrozo—then District Superintendent over the Headquarters district—and I both felt strongly about this, as did many others. So, it was absolutely amazing, later on, to come to realize that, somehow, Joe Tkach had been "maneuvered" into a position where he became Pastor General of the entire Worldwide Church of God.

In the spring of 1967, Mrs. Herbert Armstrong died—though some of us had spent *many* hours praying for her, even having meetings with Mr. Armstrong in his study where we talked about her condition and prayed for her together. God did let her go to sleep, as she was over 75 years of age when she died.

In October of 1967, my daughter Rebecca was born in a college home right next to the campus—Margie and I now had *four* children. What a responsibility! Rebecca was a beautiful and sweet child, and we always enjoyed her together, up until Margie's untimely death in 1976.

### Dr. Robert Kuhn

Another interesting and very helpful individual—whom I first knew when he was a freshman student at Ambassador College—was named Robert Kuhn. Robert was working on his doctorate at the UCLA Brain Research Institute at the same time he was attending Ambassador

College as a freshman. As we came to see that he was a very brilliant young man, we were able to use him as a Faculty Assistant and Editorial Assistant. He also helped us develop the *Tomorrow's World* magazine, which the Worldwide Church of God published from June 1969 to April 1972. Some of you will now realize *why*, in the Living Church of God, we are publishing a magazine called *Tomorrow's World*; since the title was not being used at the time and I was free to do so, I took the *same* title we had developed under Mr. Armstrong's direction for our flagship publication.

Over time, Robert and I became dear friends. We enjoyed working together, also spending many scores of hours together at lunches and dinners, including the circumcision celebration for one of his sons. He was also able to help Mr. Herbert Armstrong with research and writing regarding the "spirit in man" and related issues. Robert is truly brilliant in that area, through his own study and his research at UCLA into the ultimate capacity of the human mind. We have kept our friendship up through the years and, though Robert is not currently a member of the Living Church of God, he is still a friend and advisor of mine from time to time.

### Mr. Gerald Weston

Another outstanding and very dedicated individual came to Ambassador College during the mid-1960s. His name was Gerald Weston. He was recognized as an extremely dedicated and capable person and was sent into the ministry soon after his graduation in 1969. He served as associate pastor or pastor of congregations in Louisiana, Texas, and Michigan, then pastored several congregations in North and South Carolina, then was sent to Kansas City in July 1990. In Kansas City, he pastored what became the largest single congregation of the Global Church of God. He served in Kansas City for about ten years and did an *outstanding* job in a very challenging environment. During that time, he was made Regional Pastor over congregations in several states, and he gained the respect of many ministers and many hundreds of brethren.

After about ten years, we transferred Mr. and Mrs. Weston to Canada, where he supervised the entire Canadian Work and the local congregations in Canada, and he did an outstanding job there as well. He has a "world vision," and has helped us reach out to both China and

India and get a small Work started in each place. As you may know by now, Christ has guided me—after much prayer, study, and counsel—to designate him as our next Presiding Evangelist after my death. So, I am grateful to have him here in Charlotte at this time, and he has proved to be a very dedicated, wise, and capable individual. I will no doubt write much more about him in later installments of the autobiography, as events come to the point where he came into more prominence.

In Dusseldorf, Germany, ca. 1972–73, with Margie Meredith, John Karlson, and a West German state photographer.

**Editors' Note:** *From this point forward, we have incomplete accounts and partially told stories of Dr. Meredith's life extending into the early 1970s. The material contains obvious gaps that he intended to expand later, and is sadly not in publishable form. Dr. Meredith expressed his hope to finish a thorough and complete autobiography encompassing the scope of his event-filled lifetime, which spanned nine decades in his 87 years. But while we lament the absence of a full autobiography, we are grateful that Dr. Meredith was so consumed with doing the Work that he never found the time to fulfill this long-cherished desire. Happily, we can close his important, yet all-too-brief reminiscences with the Epilogue he, himself, prepared.*

# Epilogue
## The Big Picture

This short account of my early years is the story of one man used by God to do his part in a great Work. But there is a "big picture" into which this all fits. So, I want to remind you of a key lesson that has helped me keep the right perspective throughout my life.

### Three Parts of the Big Picture

Writing this autobiography, I thought and prayed about this over and over and came to realize that the key issue when looking at the Church of God today is to be absolutely sure of three things:

1. Where is God's *truth* being preached to the greatest degree at this time?

2. Where is God's *work* of getting out the Gospel of the Kingdom of God to the *whole* world most fully done at this time?

3. Where is the true *government* of God being taught and most fully practiced at this time?

I realize that *none* of these things have been done perfectly anywhere. But, under Mr. Armstrong's leadership, the Worldwide Church of God was continuing to do those things more fully than anywhere *else* in the world. With that in mind, I tried to be loyal to Mr.

# Epilogue

Armstrong and, most importantly, to *Jesus Christ,* who was and is the living Head of the Church of God (Ephesians 1:22-23).

In all of this, I realized that Mr. Armstrong was human—though very dedicated to God's truth. He was *slow* to act at times, but in the end he *did* act. Christ was obviously testing all of us. One thing that has helped me to understand him—to some extent—is the example of David, a man after God's own heart, for David did *much* more evil than most in the Church today; he murdered a man after committing adultery with his wife, and he tried to "cover it up" until God's prophet Nathan came to him about the situation. So, David—one of the greatest men of God of all time—was human, as Mr. Armstrong was human. Consider how Mr. Armstrong handled problems with his son, Garner Ted. He loved his son and went the furthest he could before finally dealing with the situation. Though Mr. Armstrong was used by God for decades, he did, in fact, *deeply* love his son and put *many* of us to the test by being so slow to finally "take care" of Ted's situation. But he did take care of it. I have always been grateful that I stayed the course and tried to be loyal to the human leader in the Work, for I knew Christ *was* in charge overall.

May God help all of us to constantly see the "big picture," keep our eyes on the living Christ, and *never* turn aside, never giving up on God in any way, for we *all* need to be involved in doing His Work and getting His message to the world as we are commanded to do. I pray that this early part of my life will be a blessing and a help to all of you longtime brethren, young people, and even new brethren to better understand the history behind this Work, what Ambassador College was really like in the early days, and what Mr. Armstrong was like—and, hopefully, help you also to see the big picture more fully than you might otherwise.

And for your own *good,* please remember that all of you who are called to be full members of God's Kingdom someday will go through *trials* and tests beyond what you may even imagine today. You—as I did—will have to face situations where everything is not perfect and yet you have to discern where God is primarily working and where you can best serve Him at any particular time. *You* will have to be big-minded enough to realize that God has never had perfect human beings to work with, except for Jesus Christ. When we think of the various foibles of the forefathers such as Jacob, outstanding leaders such as King David of Israel, and many, many others, it is obvious that God has to look at the *heart* and He discerns who is truly serving Him with sincerity and dedication in *spite* of human weaknesses. So, again, for *your* own good, try not to be too judgmental about the fact that Mr. Armstrong and many of His servants in this Work have had human nature, as I have described. Almighty *God* is truly in charge overall, and He will guide His Church and do His Work through us human beings in spite of our human weaknesses.

Finally, I would be remiss if I did not refer you to three key sources that will help fill out the whole picture of how God built His Work and Church in modern times. First, obviously, is Mr. Herbert W. Armstrong's own two-volume *Autobiography*. Second, the wonderful booklet written by Mr. John Ogwyn entitled *God's Church Through the Ages*. Third, the far more detailed volume *The Incredible History of God's True Church* by Ivor Fletcher. Like human beings, none of these works are perfect. But if you can buy or borrow these books, *do* so. They will provide many details that I am not able to include here.

A reflective moment touring East Berlin, July 1972

# Afterword

## The Legacy of Roderick C. Meredith
### *by Richard F. Ames*

The Bible's faith chapter, Hebrews 11, catalogues the lives of faithful men and women from biblical times. In the modern era of the Church, we also meet men and women of faith—many of them described in the two-volume *Autobiography of Herbert W. Armstrong*. And now, in what Dr. Roderick C. Meredith intended to be the first volume of a much longer autobiography, we have been able to read many examples of God's direction not only in Dr. Meredith's life, but also in the lives of those around him—Mr. Herbert W. Armstrong and many others. Through Dr. Meredith's recollections, we have read powerful testimony of God's guidance in the development of His Church, as Dr. Meredith did his part in preaching the Gospel and "building the Work," as he put it.

Dr. Meredith's life saw him taking part in a variety of historic trials and challenges, as we have read in these pages—from the tragic death of Mr. Dick Armstrong to the inspiring healing of the quadriplegic Howard Clark. These powerful reminiscences should give us encouragement as we face our own trials and sufferings. What major lessons can we learn from these testimonies? One theme Dr. Meredith illustrated and exemplified was his desire to follow Mr. Armstrong's example of wholehearted commitment. As Dr. Meredith has written elsewhere, the chief characteristic of all converted servants of God—the facet of character that most clearly identifies them as deeply dedicated Christians—is that they have been "conquered by God." That means a complete surrender of one's heart and mind to Christ and the

# The Autobiography of Roderick C. Meredith

Father—and a continuing and persevering life of service, love, and dedication.

Working so closely with Mr. Armstrong over the years, Dr. Meredith saw Mr. Armstrong's "human frailties" up close like few others. And I, as "Rod's brother-in-law," saw his human weaknesses—as I know he saw mine. But he never stopped fighting them, never surrendered to his frailties. In his last few years, especially after the debilitating stroke he suffered in September 2008 and his battle with cancer at the end of his life, he prayed fervently and consistently that God would not just help him continue to do the Work, but also help him learn whatever lessons he needed to learn before he died. That is a powerful example for each of us, as we all need to learn lasting lessons of life as God guides us daily in our walk with Him.

Dr. Meredith's strong godly will, along with his deep faith in Jesus Christ as the active Head of the Church, sustained him through many trials and challenges in the years beyond what this incomplete autobiography covers. We are grateful that he incorporated the Global Church of God in December 1992, providing a "way of escape" for thousands of brethren while the Worldwide Church of God was quickly abandoning old truths and proclaiming many apostate doctrines. Later he endured another schism, establishing the Living Church of God in November 1998. Remarkably, despite the disruption of almost "starting from scratch" again in the Living Church of God, he was back on the air with an internationally broadcast television program, *Tomorrow's World,* just six weeks after the rebellion by some of the Global leaders took him off the air. I was grateful for the opportunity to support him as a fellow *Tomorrow's World* presenter, and before long he added Mr. John Ogwyn, Mr. Rod King, and others whom he both nurtured and inspired as powerful presenters. As I write this, the *Tomorrow's World* telecast airs weekly on scores of television stations and the *Tomorrow's World* magazine reaches more than 500,000 English-language subscribers, with many thousands more in at least three other languages.

Dr. Meredith's autobiography details just a small part of his vibrant and exciting life. But he wanted us to appreciate all of Church history. As you have just read, he encouraged brethren to discover more of the history of the Church, giving special recommendation to the two-volume autobiography of Mr. Armstrong, to *God's Church*

# Afterword

*Through the Ages* by John Ogwyn, and to *The Incredible History of God's True Church* by Ivor Fletcher.

 Dr. Meredith served effectively and faithfully for more than 64 years as an evangelist of Jesus Christ. His many articles, sermons, campaigns, baptizing tours, and radio and television programs testify to the power of Jesus Christ working with him and through him, as do his decades of college and church administration.

 Yet he was much more than Church "history." My brother-in-law Rod was a loving family man as well. He enjoyed family dinners and get-togethers, and he kept up with the activities of his children, grandchildren, and great-grandchildren. He was a loving husband to his first wife, the former Margie McNair, who died of cancer in June 1976, and to his second wife, the former Sheryl Ringer, who died of cancer in November 2013.

 All of us who knew him look forward to seeing Dr. Meredith again at the resurrection of God's faithful servants at Jesus Christ's return. Until then, we are grateful that God inspired Dr. Meredith to appoint as his successor Mr. Gerald E. Weston, who in serving as the present Presiding Evangelist of the Living Church of God carries on not just the legacy of Dr. Meredith, but also the legacy of Mr. Armstrong and many other faithful servants of Jesus Christ. Mr. Weston often admonishes us, as did Dr. Meredith, to always keep our eyes on the "big picture," for we have one of the greatest God-given missions anyone could have—to preach the Gospel of the Kingdom of God to all nations, to warn Israelite nations and the world of the coming Great Tribulation, to "feed the flock" of brethren God calls, and to prepare the world and the Church for Jesus Christ's soon-coming return as King of kings and Lord of lords.

 May God bless you, dear readers, as you strive to follow in Dr. Meredith's footsteps as he followed in the footsteps of Mr. Armstrong and—ultimately and most vitally—of Jesus Christ.